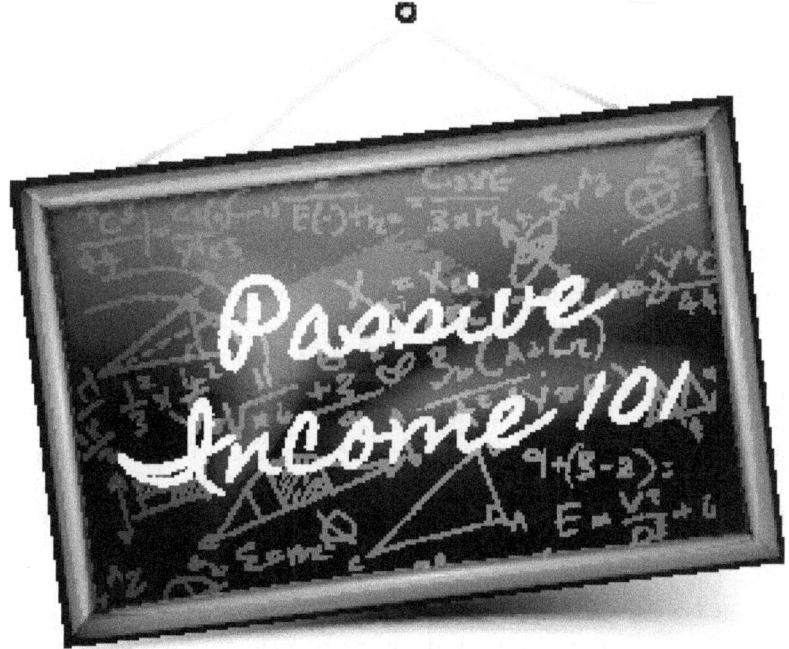

A Story of Paying for College Without Selling Your Soul

by
Sandy Shepard

Copyright © 2013 Sandra J. Shepard. All Rights Reserved.

No part of this book may be reproduced, scanned, or distributed in any printed, mechanical or electronic form (including recording or photocopying) without written permission, except in the case of brief quotations embodied in critical articles or reviews. Please do not participate in or encourage piracy of copyrighted materials in violation of the author's rights. Please only purchase authorized editions. This book is a work of fiction; if you think a character is good and you like the character, it's you. If you think the character is awful and you think it's someone you know, it's not. Fiction. Made up. Not real people (except of course Robert Kiyosaki, Jordan Adler, and other motivational speakers/authors listed). Every effort has been made to ensure that the information contained in this book is complete and accurate. However, neither the publisher nor the author is rendering professional advice or services to the individual reader. Neither the author nor the publisher shall be liable or responsible for any loss or damage allegedly arising from any information or suggestion in this book. Rich Dad and the Cashflow Quadrant are the registered trademarks of CASHFLOW Technologies, Inc. Beach Money is the trademark of Exit Strategy, Inc. All typographical and grammatical errors are here on purpose, because some people look for them and we want to please as many people as possible.

Mollydooker Press
3151 Airway Ave, Suite K-205
Costa Mesa CA 92626
United States

Dedication

To you . . .

This book is dedicated to the AMAZING person
you already are.

And the even more AMAZING person
you are becoming.

I hope that this gives you some ideas;
makes you think.

Enjoy.

Acknowledgements

Many thanks . . .

To Dawn McD. For the hand up.
To Tommy W. For the handshake.
To Og Mandino. For teaching through tales.
To my team. For everything.

Contents

Chapter One 1
Chapter Two 5
Chapter Three 9
Chapter Four 11
Chapter Five 19
Chapter Six 29
Chapter Seven 33
Chapter Eight 43
Chapter Nine 47
Chapter Ten 53
Chapter Eleven 57
Chapter Twelve 65
Chapter Thirteen 75
Chapter Fourteen 87
Chapter Fifteen 95
Chapter Sixteen 101
Chapter Seventeen 105
Chapter Eighteen 113
Chapter Nineteen 119
Chapter Twenty 123
Chapter Twenty-One 135
Chapter Twenty-Two 139
Epilogue 145
List of Resources 149
About The Author 150

Testimonials

"As a high school guidance counselor with over 22 years' experience and a Masters in counseling, I picked up Passive Income 101 with interest, especially given its subtitle. This issue is a hot one! Although I'm not currently affiliated with network marketing, I enjoyed Sandy's writing style and the message of the book. I particularly liked that she encouraged pursuing two dreams:

1. Financial success by owning your own business and earning income through supporting and helping others, while
2. Believing that a college degree is important – and that it's OK to start at a community college.

We all deserve and are capable of financial security. Passive Income 101 allows younger people to read a story in their voice that is both interesting and relevant. I look forward to recommending it to my students, and perhaps their parents too."

—*Greg Gmahling, Guidance Counselor, Vacaville High School*

"A must-read for the person seeking financial freedom and an alternative to working a 9-to-5 job! Sandy provides a modern, fresh look into how we can create financial independence while building a legacy and living the American Dream. Passive Income 101 provides a very modern and 'relatable' perspective into the home-based business industry."

—*Sheri Henderson*
Senior Sales Director, Mary Kay®
SheriHenderson.com

"My passion and mission is to help college students get not only the most out of college but also the most out of life. That's what my community DormRoomWealth.com is all about. When I was in college, I was in sports, worked as an R.A., had good grades (and had fun too, don't get me wrong), but I always had in the back of my head that I'd need to get a "G.O.O.D." ("Get Out Of Debt" as Alexzandra says in the book) job when I was through. Then, like her, I had an 'epiphany' after reading Robert Kiyosaki's books and having my dad tell me we didn't have enough money to keep me in college, 3 semesters from the end. Although this book is told from a female's perspective, I was with Alexzandra every step of the way. If I'd had this in high school, I would have gotten on this path earlier. I strongly recommend Passive Income 101 to the DormRoomWealth.com community, perhaps for younger brothers or sisters still at home who are wondering...where am I going? What am I doing? And most importantly, how am I going to make money and live my passion?"

—Curtis Lewsey
Network Marketing Leader / Master Trainer / Eagle Distributor;
Founder and Chief Motivational Officer, DormRoomWealth.com
Co-author, Appreciation Marketing™;
How to Achieve Greatness Through Gratitude

"There is a better way. You can create the life you dream of, and Passive Income 101 shows people both young and old that you don't need to follow the crowd to be successful. This book is a page-turner and will have you inspired to follow your dreams, and think outside the box. Every high school student and parent of high school students should read this book."

—Adam Packard
Network marketing professional (AdamPackard.com);
Author of Stay the Course

"From the time I started to read Passive Income 101, I found it was witty, entertaining and incredibly real. Sandy Shepard has captured the true essence of the thoughts of not only a teenager of today, but also 35+ parents who have been through enough experience to realize that working for a Corporation or being self-employed isn't all that you thought it would be. I enjoyed the mix between a teenager's view and the adult view points, all while being entertained with the everyday activities of school, work and home life. Bob and I have been married for 42 years and are proud parents and grandparents, and truly can say that times have surely changed...and it's about time! Passive Income 101 also guides you without you even realizing it in the fine art of how to be successful in an MLM company. I highly recommend this as a pre-requisite to starting your MLM business...no matter which one you choose!"

—*Betty Ann Golden*
Bob and Betty Ann Golden, top earners in their MLM for the past seven years;
Master Trainers / Eagle Distributors / MLM Professionals

"Passive Income 101 is destined to become an important work in the network marketing profession. Sandy captures so much of what network marketing is all about, through a clever and entertaining story. On the surface, it seems to be geared towards teenagers and twenty-somethings, but it's as important—if not more important— for their parents. I almost felt myself reliving my own network marketing journey in many ways."

—*Tommy Wyatt*
Network Marketing Leader / Master Trainer / Eagle Distributor
Co-author, Appreciation Marketing™;
How to Achieve Greatness Through Gratitude

Chapter One

"OK, FINE Mom!" I said, hanging up from the call and rolling my eyes to the tiled ceiling outside my Math class. I mean, really. Math is bad enough, and her call about my college applications didn't help. She'd given me a break for my birthday yesterday, but now it was all back—full press stress.

I walked down the hall towards English, texting my BFF Stephanie, turning my shoulders left or right to avoid the crowds of other students, without looking up from the screen.

"Aikido texting again, Alex?"

I glanced up just before running into my brother, Charlie. Well, he's not really my brother. But our moms have been best friends since they dropped us off at the kindergarten bus stop, so he kinda is.

"Shut UP," I said with a laugh. "I just let their Force pass me by. It's a Jedi thing." My mom had worked as a lawyer at Lucasfilm; guess I use old Star Wars metaphors by osmosis.

"So…?" I said as he dropped into step next to me, "What up?"

Just as he was opening his mouth, my phone pinged with Stephanie's answer. I checked it, laughed, and hit her back. I could feel Charlie rolling his eyes.

"I'm listening, I'm listening!" I said. "Swear." I slid the phone into the back pocket of my jeans. "Look! Hands!" I said, holding my palms up as we both laughed.

"So your mom told MY mom…."

"OK your next sentence better not include the words 'admission' or 'application' or 'college'," I warned, and he paused.

"Alex, look. I know it sucks, but you know it's important. College is the only way to get where you want."

I felt the phone vibrate in my pocket, but resisted the temptation to answer. Barely.

"Seriously—what are your options? Your mom's a lawyer, your dad does sales, my dad's a doctor, mom's got the shop. Who makes more? Who's safer? Your mom. My dad. The lawyer and the doctor. Seriously," he said again, stopping in front of his AP Calc class. I gave him my 'you're nagging like my mother' look.

"OK," he said, "Sure, your mom had that stuff happen between being general counsel and now, and Dad sometimes can't get to my track meets because of an emergency. But look. You say you want to do good; we talk about all your ideas about horses for special needs kids and training dogs, or dolphins, or revitalizing Hawaiian traditions or whatever. Oh, and all while living on the beach, of course. If you're going to do that, you have to get a degree. You have to get a good job and excel and save—all the boring-but-necessary stuff. You can't have your dreams and have money and be safe. It's not realistic. Maybe you can send donations to a dolphin-dog-horse-special-needs-Hawaiian-language foundation. Maybe… whatever. Get a timeshare in Kauai like we have, go every other year. But look, you have to…well, you have to, like, face it."

He smiled his 'no hard feelings' smile and the corners of my lips turned up in response, but I rolled my eyes. My stomach hurt just thinking about it. I didn't even really know what I wanted yet, and it felt like everybody was forcing me to plan my whole life already.

"Meet you in the Quad for break?" he said, disappearing behind the classroom door, then peeked back out quickly. "Oh—and Happy Birthday yesterday," he said, and ducked back in before I could say anything.

I moved back into the crush to get to Miss Young's room for English. Before surrendering my phone to her *No Phone Zone* shelf, I slid my backpack down off my shoulder and pulled the phone from my pocket to find out what juicy tidbit Stephanie had sent while I was talking to Charlie. Josh was in front of me, keying feverishly. He was brilliant at the technical stuff—especially for pranking. Yesterday his phone interrupted class by belting out a strip tease. Today though, Miss Young pointed to a new sign that said, 'Prove Your Phone Is Off.' Kelly, her freakin' lackey, was standing by the shelf making sure our phones were actually dead. Josh groaned and handed over his phone. I looked down to catch the text on my phone before powering down. That's odd—something must be wrong. The text was from ALEX-MOBILE—from me. How could that be? But it wasn't some random butt-dial, because it said:

        YDKM but WDR
  U can hv ur drms n $$ n safety
          Uni z NTOW

Chapter Two

Kelly held out her palm and I hit the Off button, handing her my phone as I walked past. Where did that come from? How could it say it was from me? In a daze, I nearly tripped over Josh's foot on my way to my desk, thinking about what I'd read on my phone.

You don't know me, but with due respect...

I couldn't figure out how the texter had used my and Stephanie's shorthand. Stephanie and I had invented a Secret Language back in grammar school, probably like third grade. That way we could talk and no one would know what we were talking about. Once we got our phones, we did the same with the text shorthand. Most everyone had shortcuts built into their phones so they would type "IMO" and it would print "in my opinion"–but Steffie and I had just stuck with a mix of our secret code and some old text acronyms no one really used any more.

Luckily, my mind could wander, because today we were just continuing our play-act-read of *Hamlet*, one of Miss Young's favorite oldies. I only had a bit part in the 'Play Within A Play,' which we weren't likely to get to until tomorrow. I watched the words on the page as our class hams read the old Bard. Actually, usually I liked it, but today I couldn't even pay attention to the great Ophelia that Randy Taless could pull off.

I sneaked a peek at my phone lying dead on the shelf. I wanted to take a look at the numbers on the text—how could it have said that it was coming from the phone itself? Something was up. I'd have to ask Dad whether a cloned phone would show my number—but who would clone me, then text me? Worse, it had to be someone who was walking and listening to Charlie and me upstairs—given the subject of the text—which creeped me out.

> ...you can have your dreams & money & safety.
> University is not the only way.

And besides—who would think that? Everybody knows college is just the next step after high school to start your life.

OK, I know I was moaning about going to college, but I'm a good kid. I'm going. Sure, I wanted to agree with the texter, but what other choice is there? Work retail? That's certainly not the path to riches. Babysit? Mow lawns? For life?

The thing that gets me about higher education is that it's not over at four years. You have to go to basically a trade school, either after high school or after college to learn how to "be" anything—a cosmetologist, a lawyer, a doctor, a real estate agent, whatever. Our parents made college the new high school. Anyone who was anyone found a way to go. Now you're a slacker if you don't. But did it really prepare you for the real world? Too many of my friends' older brothers and sisters were college grads, but still lived at home and worked at the same jobs as kids in high school.

I don't even really know what I want to do. I mean, I'm not a wiz at anything. I'm not cutting myself down. I can carry a tune, I do fine in school. I don't really bug anyone enough to get picked on, but I'm not in the super popular crowd either. I have your standard, run-of-the-mill ideas and dreams. I'm not a math geek like Charlie or have that powerful charisma of someone like Randy; I don't have super stage fright, but I'm not in debate club, either. I don't seem to have what my dad extols as the 'entrepreneurial spirit'—I'm not the girl who had the lemonade stand in grade school or found balls at the golf course then sold them for money. But I'm a good listener, a great babysitter actually, probably because I really like people—all people. Old, young, in between. And I generally have a good attitude (my earlier call with Mom notwithstanding). But how do you make a college major—and a career—out of that? And I'm not even sure if having a 'career' be the be-all and end-all of my life—like our folks did—really matters.

In my crowd, the talk is always about what is 'real.' And for most of my friends and me, what would actually make a difference to the world. In the work/study stuff we had to go through, the jobs that the counselors said would always be there were things like nursing and sales, if they thought you weren't the doctor/lawyer type and liked people—maybe military if you didn't. Then it was all engineering, government jobs…even teaching if you took a perverse pleasure in being paid nothing to basically have kids ignore you…

I suddenly realized that the room was silent and a little expectant. Josh turned back to me from his desk, waving the fingers of his right hand slowly in front of his face and obviously repeating, in a "Hell-ooooo" slow voice what I had just missed:

"For…HUSBAND…shalt…thou…"

I started in my seat, sat up, and flipped two pages forward, to my lines as the Player Queen. How'd I get two pages behind?

"O, confound the rest!" I recited, as Josh, the Player King, turned back with a smirk. "O confound" is right—time to get with the program and pull myself together. I didn't need a random phantom text to blow my grade on this—I only had 14 lines!

"…Such love must needs be treason in my breast!"

Chapter Three

We got through the 'Play Within A Play' without any other mishaps. Picking up our phones, Josh snorted and poked fun at my "visit to the astral plane" during class. I turned my phone back on and headed for the Quad, still pondering the text I'd received right before class. Once the phone was on, a bunch of other texts came in—one from Stephanie, a couple others—but I scrolled back down. Sure enough, there it was, and it came from ALEX-MOBILE—in other words, from me. I took another look:

> You don't know me, but with due respect,
> you can have your dreams & money & safety.
> University is not the only way.

I saw Charlie as soon as I hit the bar on the door to get out to the Quad; he was hanging with his track buddies. He nodded to me, and we headed over to one of the benches.

"What do you make of this?" I said without preamble, handing him my phone.

He studied the text, then looked at me, then back at the phone.

"Y.D.K'em? N-Tow?" he said, which cracked me up. I forgot—Charlie isn't much of a texter, much less understanding Steffie and my shorthand.

"It says 'You don't know me'—that's the **YDKM** part. Then **WDR**—'with due respect'—'you can have your dreams and money and safety'—**Uni**—'University'—is **NTOW**—'not the only way.'"

"Someone was obviously listening to us—that's actually kinda creepy."

"Well, yeah but the thing is—look where it's from. It's from me."

Charlie tilted his head, raising one eyebrow and tucking his chin in—the universal "Whaaaat?" look.

"OK, you're right. That's just odd. You should ask your dad who could've done that." Though my dad's in sales, he's definitely Mr. Techie. "Or, well," he continued, "What if you answer it?"

I hadn't thought of that. "What would I say?"

"Just ask what they want…what can it hurt? They obviously heard us. It might be that one of the computer lab geeks likes you and is trying to get your attention."

"By cloning my phone? Now that's a sure way to get a date." We laughed. "What should I say?"

"What about just 'What do you mean?' or 'Come on suckah show yourself and speak in person like a man'… What's that in 'Text'?"

I snorted, thought for a second, and just went with it and responded,

WDYM

Chapter Four

By the time I got home, I was pretty much over it. My WDYM—"What do you mean?"—text had gone unanswered. Obviously whoever had done it didn't want to keep up the conversation. I was still annoyed that someone had been listening in on me and Charlie…not to mention the whole 'phone cloning' thing.

I knew Mom was going to get on me to start the college applications tonight, and I knew she was right. I mean, who doesn't go to college? I was very lucky, because my folks were going to pay for it. Sure, I would get student loans, but they would pay what I couldn't cover. It was all planned for me. I had to get a "good" major—something I could "do something" with, like Economics or Business. Whatever my folks want is fine with me, because I don't really have a calling…except maybe to Hawaii.

I've never been to Hawaii, but it fascinates me. When I was about ten years old I even asked for a *Learn Hawaiian from Home* set—when tape cassettes showed up, we all laughed. I do still have it in my bookshelf, and someday I might find an old cassette tape player at a Goodwill store or, in my dreams, just learn 'on island.'

But back to that 'calling' thing. Mom knew she wanted to be a lawyer from the time she was in high school. So she went that route and seemed happy to have done it, even though, as she told it, it took years to get out from under the debt. I'd have debt too from the student loans, but only a few tens of thousands. That still sounds like a lot, but that's just what you do. And it wasn't like going out-of-state or to medical school or anything. You've got to rob a bank for that kind of money.

I felt more like my dad. He really hadn't known what he wanted to do. He was personable, so he got a sales job at his company while he paid down his college debt…then he'd just stayed. He's actually worked there for quite a while. He believes in the product, which is the kicker I think. My mom always teases him that he would have been a great litigator because he could "Sell a king-sized bed to the Pope." But from what I could gather, he hadn't been all that great in school; he was more of a jock.

I think that's why he pushes hard about good grades and a good school and really doing well in high school, to have options for a good college. He wants the best for me. If you ask me, though, I think my dad would rather be teaching surfing lessons. But I guess that's the standard thing—get married, have kids, get a house, get a mortgage, and there you are. So where do your dreams fit in?

I got an apple from the fridge and cut a sliver off the remains of my birthday cake, poking it all guiltily in my mouth as if someone might see me. I closed the refrigerator door and turned around. Sure enough, I saw the college applications set out on the kitchen table. I set up my homework on our big dark wood dining room table instead. It wasn't so much that I was ignoring the apps; it's just that if I got started, I would get pulled down into the big black hole of thinking about what each app wanted, and not get my homework done. I also knew that once Mom got home, she'd want to go through the apps, talk about what a 'good' answer could be for each essay, blah blah. If I got started in the wrong direction, I'd have to scrap it all and start over. Sure, I could go fill out my name, birth date, address—all that jazz. But for once in my life, I felt the desire to do my homework.

I was just unpacking in the dining room when my phone pinged from my back pocket. I really did need to get my stuff done before my folks got home. Believe it or not, I'm pretty good at time management. Usually I turn my phone off until everything's done, because that can be a big black hole too. But I figured I'd just check the text and shoot back that I'd be busy for a few, until I read:

bc YDK what U want 2B
ITC Uni-> -$$-> GOOD job-> B4YKI ur stuck
U need 2B B/I not E/S
C Kiyosaki YAFIYGI

The texter! Once again, it was from ALEX-MOBILE. In the shorthand. It said:

Because you don't know what you want to be—in that case, University means negative $$, which leads to a Get Out Of Debt [G.O.O.D.] job and Before You Know It, you're stuck. You need to be B/I not E/S. See Kiyosaki—You asked for it, you got it.

WHO R U

I texted. I didn't even pay attention to what had been said—I just wanted to know who had cloned my phone. This was just not funny. I scrolled back up, trying to see if there was anything I was missing—some sign pointing to who was doing this. I heard a ping, and read:

::poof::

indicating the texter was gone. I texted a couple more times just to be sure, and let's just say that if my mom understood acronyms, she would have grounded me for a week for what I said. But 'they' were gone.

I finally simmered down and started my homework. But I kept thinking about parts of this latest text, mulling it over in the back of my mind as I filled out vocabulary flashcards for language class and tried to concentrate on Math.

Because you don't know what you want to be—*It's like they could read my mind*—**in that case, University means negative $$**—*I guess that's debt*—**which leads to a Get Out Of Debt job and Before You Know It—you're stuck.** *Totally what I'd been thinking, and that creeped me out.*

I didn't get the next part of the text though. **You need to be B/I not E/S…?** B.I.? Business Intelligence? The only "E.S." I knew had been part of my text rant a couple minutes ago directed at my cyber-hacker-stalker… and I'm sure that's not what they meant. I had no clue about that one. Then, **See Kiyosaki. You asked for it, you got it.**

Kiyosaki? Sounds like some old martial arts movie. You know, go see the reclusive monk guru on the mountaintop, find your path.

Finally, I couldn't deal with it anymore. I was obsessing and couldn't concentrate, so I called my dad. Usually he's on his way home about now, and could talk in the car or on the ferry, depending on how he'd gone to work. If he'd taken the ferry, he usually filled the time that it took to get to his office and back with magazines, especially ones where he could dream up vacations for us Unfortunately, we didn't get to get away that much; something was always going on. And for the past few years, well, they'd started saving hard for me to head to college. But Dad kept planning. If he was driving, no doubt he'd be doing the 'Automobile University' thing—listening to personal development audio of some sort. I actually liked them, and sometimes dreamed I'd be a motivational speaker. To dolphins. In Hawaii. (Joking!) But seriously, they were usually filled with great advice and stories, all broken up into bite-size pieces. That's actually where he met Mom, at one of those seminars a billion years ago.

I called, and after a ring I heard his voice and some applause in the background.

"What up, Alexzandra?"

I laughed because as he was talking, I could hear a voice in the background before he turned it down. Sure enough—Automobile University.

So now I had my dad on the phone—how to broach the subject with him? I was pretty sure my folks would freak out if I said that I had some sort of cyber-stalker, who was texting me using my own number no less. It sounded like the beginning of a bad scream movie.

"How'd your day go, kiddo?"

"Not so bad," I said, buying time. Then a possible solution popped into my head. My dad knows the most esoteric things. On a hunch I said, "Hey, so. Do you know who 'Kiyosaki' is?"

My dad was silent for a couple beats. I could just see his face, his forehead sort of squishing down between his eyebrows as he tried to figure out what I was talking about.

"You mean Robert Kiyosaki?" he said. "Like *Rich Dad, Poor Dad*, E/S/B/I, all that jazz?" Then, "What?" with a little concern in his voice. His headset must be better than I thought, because he must have heard my sharp intake of breath.

"Did you say E.S.B.I.?" I asked incredulously.

"Yes, the ways to make money. We read his book a while ago, and it made a lot of sense. I just couldn't figure out how to get the whole cash flow concept into our life. I have his books in my study somewhere—you can read them if you want. It's not rocket science. How did this come up?"

I paused for a second, not really sure how to start. I figured a white lie might just be easier. I wasn't ready to freak my dad out. "There were some kids at school talking about it, talking about not going to college. I couldn't really hear all of it, but it was something to do with Kiyosaki and being B/I." I said the two letters carefully, hoping they would make sense to my dad. That part of the text was a mystery to me.

"They're talking about money. How what you really want is to be either a B—a Business—or to make money through Investments, the I. The other two ways are being an Employee, which is the E, or being Self-Employed, which is the S." I heard the turned-down voice stop, as my dad punched the Off button on his car stereo. "The whole deal with the *Rich Dad* books is that Kiyosaki had two dads. His actual father who was not rich, but ran the school system, so he wanted him to get an education and a job; and his best friend's dad, who wound up getting rich because he invested in things like a business and real estate, but didn't have much formal education. Hey—he was from Hawaii, even," Dad said, and of course that totally caught my attention.

"You know," he continued, "why don't we talk about it at dinner? Mom's coming home on time tonight, and I'm on my way. If you get your homework done, we can eat dinner together for a change, which your mom and I would really like."

"Mom's going to want to talk about the applications," I warned, pouting.

"Well, let's beat her to the punch. I think this is a great subject, and I never thought you'd be interested in anything like this. How did you get sooo smart?" he said in a singsong way, and I could hear the smile in his voice.

"Must have been Mom!" I said, hitting him with our standard comeback.

Hey, we're just an ordinary family, and we do love each other. Of course, as a teenager, sometimes I just ignore it.

"I'll be home in about an hour. Why don't you take something out for dinner and get your homework finished? Then, if you set the table, it'll be done and we can catch your mom as soon as she changes from work. Having dinner started would go a long way," he added, and I laughed—so true. Mom would love that. So I hung up the phone and went to the fridge to sort out some stuff for dinner, then went back to the dining room table to finish my homework. I wanted to be ready when Dad got home. Though I was still not happy about this cyber-cloning-texting-stalking thing, it'd just gotten a lot more interesting. I wanted to find out more.

Chapter Five

After finishing my homework, I figured I might as well get the applications started while I waited for Dad. I went into the kitchen, sat down at the breakfast table, and rifled through the stack. All the schools were in-state. We have a bunch of good schools here, and though it might have been fun to fill out a throwaway Harvard or Stanford app, there's no way I could go, even maxing out my student loans. It's easily double or triple the money if you try to go out-of-state, not even to mention a private school.

Then I remembered something. I went down to my room and snuck the University of Hawaii at Manoa application out from under my bed. I'd sent away for it myself, and since- I'm generally the one who gets the mail, no one had been the wiser. I decided to slip it into the stack. Mom had arranged them from what looked like most likely to least likely—I decided to put it right smack in the middle. Again—not a chance—out-of-state tuition was non-negotiable, and I wanted to go to the School of Hawaiian Knowledge with maybe some sort of double major in Marine Biology since they did so much work with marine mammals.

There's a combination sure to get me a job on the Wall Street path; more like the 'Would you like fries with that?' path.

After I slid it into the stack, I started on the first app. I was just finishing the general information part when I heard Dad's car in the driveway. I quickly but carefully block-printed in the last of the info for that page, so that it would at least look like I had done something. Mom's view was that I should fill the applications out on paper instead of online, because then a real person had to look at them. Mom had read a lot about the whole system, and that at some colleges, a computer could dump you without a real person even reviewing your qualifications, because you didn't shell out the big bucks for one of those consultants who knew all the current hot words used by the application scanning software.

The back screen slammed and Dad came in like he always does—what Mom calls a "big sunny tornado." My Dad has a great outlook. His hair was messed up, so he must have had the sunroof open in the car. He went straight to the fridge and opened it, surveyed, and cut a sliver of cake. He shot me a guilty smile as he threw it in his mouth like a frat boy swallowing a goldfish. Then he grabbed an apple. Like daughter, like father.

"Let me get changed and then we'll put dinner together," he said, brushing frosting off his lip with his thumb, then tossing the apple spinning into the air and catching it behind his back. He nudged the back of my head as he walked past me at the kitchen table. I had to laugh—Dad's mood is always infectious. "Working on the apps? Awesome—homework done?" I nodded and he headed to get into his sweats.

Dad and I had dinner going in full rock-and-roll mode when Mom came home, with a Genius set off Dad's iPod® playing loud as we worked. He'd started it on some old Rolling Stones—we'd moved through Led Zeppelin to The Ramones to Black Tide to Far to Green Day back to The Stones to Bon Jovi and, just as the back door squeaked open, *Last Train to Clarksville* by the Monkees started up.

"OK what—The Monkees?" Mom said as she walked into the kitchen. Then she just stopped dead and laughed. Chopped vegetables were, well, sort of everywhere, a sauté was going, and there were various herb jars open on the counter. Dad, in a 'Dinner's Ready When the Smoke Alarm Goes Off' apron, was just sliding a pan into the oven with a flourish as one foot and, yes, I'm embarrassed to say his behind, kept the beat of the song.

"Blame the Genius," I said.

Mom air-kissed Dad near the cheek he offered her sideways and said, "OK you guys, let me get changed; I'll be right back." Her heels clicked on the kitchen tile as she passed, tucking her butt in as Dad tried to pat her with his big oven-mittened paw. Sometimes they were just embarrassing. I definitely saw Mom glance, then smile, at the pile of applications on her way by. I was glad I'd started the first one and left it open.

"So, you know, I wasn't born yesterday," Mom said when she reappeared in the kitchen, just as Dad finished plating dinner. She wore a trim set of matching turquoise sweats with her hair back in a ponytail, face washed. You could see the freckles that ran across the bridge of her nose, which she covered up every morning with foundation—she said they made her look "not serious enough" for a lawyer. Dad, of course, said he liked her best this way, and I tended to agree. She picked up two of the plates and carried them to the dining room table. "And though I love the family dinner thing, and especially not to have to get it ready…spill it."

Dad smiled sheepishly, his hair falling down over his eyes as he sat down at the head of the table. That made Mom laugh. I actually thought about it for a second—though Mom and Dad sometimes ate together, Mom often had to work late, and Dad sometimes wasn't even in town, depending on what he was doing for his company. Usually I would take dinner into my room and eat it lying on my bed with the computer on my stomach. Though I'd never admit it to them, it was actually nice to sit down together.

"Alex heard some kids today talking about Kiyosaki at school, and she asked me about it," Dad began, deftly cutting a piece of his asparagus. "I said that we could talk about it at dinner."

"Kiyosaki?" Mom said, taking a bite. "Robert Kiyosaki? Man—Steve—it's been a while since I've thought about that," she said. She turned her bright green eyes at me. "What was the gist of what they were saying, and what got you interested?"

I felt a little weird being back in white lie mode. If I told them the phone thing, Kiyosaki would be totally off the table. "It was basically about the B.S.I. thing," I said, trying to remember the letters.

"E/S/B/I? The Cashflow Quadrant?" said Mom, and I nodded. She nodded lightly, putting down her fork as she thought. "Kiyosaki has been criticized since he wrote that book, and a lot of people don't want to see the value or relevance of it," she said, my dad nodding with her. "Your father and I read *Rich Dad, Poor Dad*, and I remember how excited we were." She smiled and was silent for a second, lost in thought. "In fact, it all started because I was working in-house at that Internet startup, which was kind of on shaky ground." My guess was that this was the one that had popped with the Internet bubble, sending her back to the law firm after trying to go out on her own for a while. "I had a friend at the gym who suggested Kiyosaki's books," she said, and she and Dad both nodded again, neither one eating, just remembering.

"Your dad and I got the *Rich Dad, Poor Dad* book, and the *Cashflow* board game at her suggestion. We realized we'd never really thought about money that way. The E.S./B.I. comes from Kiyosaki's book *The Cashflow Quadrant*. He says there are four basic ways to make money, and two are better than the others when it comes to getting financially free. Being an E-Employee means you're working for 'The Man,' as the saying goes. You're not building your life, you're building their company. And you could work harder, or more hours, but at the end of the day, your fortunes really are out of your hands." I thought about Mom being "right-sized" as the euphemism was back then (in other words, laid off), and I was pretty sure that's what both she and Dad were thinking about, too. "The S is for Self-Employed—your dad actually said that being an S means that you're workin' for The Man—and The Man is YOU!" Dad snorted a little laugh at that. That sounded like him.

"Meaning that you think that you have a business, which is the B, but in reality, you have to do everything. You leave it, you get sick—you don't get paid. It seems like you can make more than being an E—because you're not tied to a certain salary and all that. But in reality, if you stop working, the money stops coming in. *And* you're the marketing department, the payroll department, the worker bee, the janitor, and everything else all rolled up into one. A true B-Business is like Stephanie's dad," she said, taking a sip from her glass. "He runs their business, but if he steps away, it keeps going and throwing off money for him and their family. And Stephanie and her sister will inherit it. With being an S, because what you do is specialized—say like a lawyer or consultant for example—you can't just delegate it and go on vacation, or transfer it to your kids without them becoming a clone of you. Depending on what you do, that can take years, if it happens at all."

"Is that like what happened with your law firm you started?" I asked.

"Sort of," she said. "I had lots of clients, because folks I'd worked with at the software company before I tried the 'dot bomb' all knew me, and wanted me to do their law work when they started out on their own. But when the economy tightened up, folks' dreams seemed to crawl into a hole and die. Most of them scurried back to being employees—if they could find jobs at all. So I had to work harder to get business, but I also had to worry about collections. I ended up taking unreasonable clients I might have turned down before, just to make ends meet."

I remembered making some extra money being her 'collections agency,' making calls to some of her real deadbeat clients to try to get payment plans going. Not fun. Ultimately, she wound up going back into a law firm, where she had colleagues, benefits, a more stable salary, and someone else chasing down the deadbeats! But she worked just as many hours, if not more, and had to deal with what she called "the vagaries of office politics." In Kiyosaki-speak, she was back being an "E."

Mom was continuing her story. "Your dad and I thought long and hard about how we could have a B-Business or get some I-Investing going, so that we could have the Holy Grail that Kiyosaki talks about—passive income. Income that comes in even if you're not working—cash flow."

"How can money come in when you're not working?" I asked, a little puzzled. Dad took it from there, pushing back his empty plate and rocking the two front legs of his chair off the ground. Mom gave him The Look for that, which he pretended to ignore, taking a sip from his glass as he picked up the tale.

"Well, think about it. There's rent, for example, if you own a rental house. As long as the rent is more than your mortgage and taxes and such, it creates cash flow. Or if you write a song, book, or a movie, like your mom's clients, you get residuals into the future. It's basically doing some work on the front end which leads to a flow of money on the back end." He got his sheepish smile again and shook his head side to side, rolling his eyes.

"In fact, we investigated all sorts of potential investments—trying to figure out things like storage facilities, or Laundromats, and your mom even got into an MLM, but we had to do all that while we were working our jobs. There just wasn't enough time, and frankly, neither of us was particularly good at the math that you needed for some of the investments. We took classes, tried to figure out 'cash-on-cash' and 'net asset value' and stuff—took a class on tax liens…" at this point Mom was even shaking *her* head and rolling *her* eyes, "…but it was all way more work than we could handle. We thought about buying a franchise—like a Subway sandwiches or 7-Eleven or a Hallmark store—but the upfront franchise fees are huge, even though it does give you a system to follow. If one of us had been stay-at-home or if we had a big chunk of change, maybe. So here we are, full circle, back to being a couple'a E's," he said, snorting a little. "Maybe you should check Kiyosaki's books out. They're in my study, and they're fairly easy reads."

I thought about what he'd said. "MLM?" I said. "I get the rest, but what's that?"

"Multilevel marketing," Mom said, picking up my plate and hers, and backing through the door into the kitchen. "It's where a company uses people to tell other people about products, and then pays them if the other people buy the product, and if they sign on to promote the product themselves."

I considered that as she cleared off the tablemats and Dad carried his empty plate into the kitchen. "So you recommend something, and get paid for recommending it—if they buy it?" I asked, leaning my back against the counter next to the fridge. Mom took the cake out and cut three pieces. Dad and I did our best not to look guilty about our previous 'tastes.' "That sounds shady."

"Actually, not so much," said Dad, filling the kettle with water. "Think about it—let's say that you see a movie that you really like. Do you go and tell Charlie and Stephanie and everyone about it?"

"Well, sure."

"And then they go—and maybe you even go again. And then they tell people who tell people."

I nodded—I wasn't sure where this was going.

"And the movie theater owner gives you a check for recommending the movie, and all the popcorn and drinks and such that everyone buys, right?" he asked, and of course I laughed.

"Not a chance."

"But they are there because of you, right?"

I nodded. Hmm.

Dad continued, "That's the thing with multilevel marketing. The idea is that a company has a product that people really like—that fills some sort of a need. Instead of spending a ton of money on advertising, they use real people and offer incentives to help get the word out. Sure, sometimes these folks are looking for a fast buck, but on the whole they really like that product and think it would be beneficial for others, too. So, if they tell people about the product and then those people buy the product, they get a piece of the sale—for introducing it. And if the product is as good as they feel it is, the people not only use it, but maybe introduce it to other people. If they do that, they get a little incentive—a check. That's why it's called 'cash flow' income—because the income 'flows' in whether you're working or not, so long as those folks buy the product or introduce others to it. In a good MLM or direct sales company, there is a system that they train you on—since you're their sales force. So it's a bit like a franchise, but the investment is just a few hundred dollars instead of thousands. Believe it or not, as an industry it's made more millionaires out of regular folks than any other, bar none."

I thought about this for a second. "What kind of products?"

"Oh, a lot of products are sold this way," Mom said as she stacked the plates into the dishwasher. "Some you have for sure heard of—like Mary Kay or Avon cosmetics. When I was a kid, my Mom's friends would have Tupperware parties—and you've probably seen me going to candle or jewelry parties. There are some cooking gadget ones, juice, vitamins, weight loss, greeting cards, phone service, stuff like that."

"So you go to a party, get together with your friends, try out stuff, then buy it—and the person who sold it gets a check?" I asked, making sure I understood.

"Yes, in a party-based MLM or dual marketing system," said Dad. "But actually, that was the problem when your mom tried this business. She got into an MLM where she loved the product and she loved introducing it to other people." I could see Mom smiling and shaking her head as she put the last of the glassware into the washer, as Dad continued. "But she knew so *much* about the product, that she wasn't able to build a team. She made what we were thinking was great money by selling products at these parties—buying it at her 40% discount, selling it at the retail price, but at the end of the day, all she was doing was being an S, not a B."

S was Self-employed, B was Business. I got it—she was spending her time to get money—but all that money came in because of her efforts, not tied to the efforts of others.

"I really did love the product, and I loved doing it," she said, "but your dad's right. All I was doing was the law during the day, and this was when I had my own firm so I was already an S, then doing in-house parties during the evening. I knew so much about what I was selling, but I wasn't 'duplicatable,' which is one of the most important things in an MLM—building a team. You have to have an uncomplicated system so that people at a party or whoever you introduce the business to can imagine themselves doing it, too. Although folks came away super informed, no one felt that they could possibly know all I knew and sell the product themselves. So ultimately, I realized it just wasn't working as we'd planned, and I wound up getting out of it. It was cutting into our personal time, too," she added.

The kettle sang. Dad turned off the burner then poured hot water over two mugs containing Tazo Wild Sweet Orange teabags—their 'wind down' drink. He raised his eyebrow at me, and I nodded; he took down another mug and opened up another tea bag. "Your mom gets excited about something and has to know everything about it—break it down into pieces. She loves to educate others. But the thing is, though she is seriously the best teacher, it's in a way that anyone listening thinks, 'Dang, that's awesome, I totally get that, but I could never remember all that myself.'"

Mom stood over at the kitchen table, now that everything was tidied up from dinner. She took the mug from Dad, but instead of heading into the study with him, she took two plates of cake over to the kitchen table and pulled out a chair and gestured to usher me into it. "Dad said your homework's done, so it's time to get some of these applications going."

I slumped into the chair, cradling the hot mug. So much for avoiding the applications for another night. My mind was still turning over what we'd been talking about. Cash flow, huh?

Chapter Six

"So what'd they say?"

Charlie stepped into the crowd with me as I walked to my locker between classes.

"Hunh?" I said, this time not because I was texting, but actually because I was thinking about last night with Mom and Dad. How had so much happened in less than 24 hours? I hadn't slept much.

"The stalker? The phone clone. What'd your parents say?"

I looked at Charlie, and he suddenly looked horrified. No poker face, this boy.

"Do not. Tell me. You did not. Tell them." He said, stopping dead in the pre-class rush and risking serious student-crash damage. I pulled on the side of his jacket, urging him out of his heel-scorching stop in the middle of the hall.

"I didn't exactly tell them," I said, turning away from him to work the combination on my locker. "I was going to, but then I got another text message that I didn't understand, so I asked Dad about what it meant—it actually meant something. Then Mom and Dad and I talked about that, and then I was doing applications." I banged the locker closed, now loaded down with books for the next three classes. "I even had the Hawaii app in there, and though Mom said I'd have to pay the application fee out of my own money, she agreed to let me do it."

"*Please,*" said Charlie, his back to the locker next to mine, blocking my way and obviously not happy. About my University of Hawaii application? I was puzzled. A couple of the girls a few lockers down gave him The Eye—Charlie might be a looker, don't ask me, he's my brother. "Please. Puh-leeeeze tell me you told your mom," he said. Then suddenly, I knew.

"Oh no—you did *not*," I said, maybe a little loudly. Maybe it turned a couple heads.

Charlie hung his head.

I was going to be in a world of hurt.

He had mentioned the whole cyber-stalker thing to his mom.

"Alex I swear I thought you would tell them this whole thing last night!" Charlie shot back, but his voice cracked. That was the telltale sign he knew that he had broken the Friend Code. With our moms, you could not say anything that wouldn't zip down the grapevine at warp speed.

I rolled my eyes. He looked totally sick to his stomach, so I decided to let him off the hook. A little.

"Look, you couldn't've known," I sighed, which at least brought his slumped head back up. "OK so this is what happened," I said, as we headed down the hall toward my class, and the stairs to his. "I got home and did my homework, or, well, right as I put my homework out, I got a text. I looked. It was from Stalkerella. I asked a question and got an answer, but then they were gone." I handed my phone over to Charlie so he could see the messages, walking a bit in front to block him from the student flow. Lockers slammed, people laughed, the hall noise was the usual roar. But I knew that he didn't hear any of it as he scrolled through my screen. "So, anyway, I called Dad. I was freaked, but I wanted to know what the long text meant, too." Charlie arched one eyebrow. (I wish I could do that.)

"So, what happened?" He handed the phone back to me. I figured he couldn't decipher that text.

"Well basically I said to Dad that I had 'heard' about Kiyosaki and the E/S/B/I part—you did see that part, right?" I said, gesturing to the phone with my eyes, and he nodded. "Dad got started on the whole subject. In fact, he and Mom talked about the whole thing—it was wild. No, seriously," I said, to Charlie's 'wha-hunh?' look. "We had dinner together and we actually talked about passive income, things like that. Then after, Mom wanted to do the apps. Seriously, I know you can't believe this, but I forgot. I really forgot how I got on the subject. Dad even gave me this book." I pulled my backpack forward off my shoulder, unzipped the top and held up the copy of *Rich Dad, Poor Dad* from Dad's study. "Then this morning, I realized that this text came in some time during dinner or later—I'd turned my phone off." I held the phone out for him to read it.

"OK text-linguist, what's it say?" We had gotten to the stairwell going up to his class. Charlie leaned his side against the wall to brace against the flow heading up and down, me on the inside. I looked at it again:

> Props 2 U 4 talking 2 th rents.
> MLM z no 2G2BT.
> Blv me. G4i. PS Not stalkin. Swear

"It basically says 'Congratulations for talking to your parents; multilevel marketing isn't too good to be true, believe me. Go for it. And by the way, I'm not stalking you, I swear'."

Charlie ignored the MLM part, latching straight onto the end of the text. "He's in your house?" Charlie said, his voice rising. "He's *in your house?!*" He said again, turning heads and making folks rounding the corner give him a wide berth.

"I'm still trying to figure it out. OK so," I lowered my voice, "what if this is like, a text angel or something?" I closed my eyes, expecting him to blow up. The roar of the hallway kept up, lockers banging, people hollering, but Charlie was silent. With my eyes closed, I could almost feel his eyes boring down on me.

I peeked. His eyes were actually staring at the ceiling. I closed mine again. Tight.

"You did not just say 'text angel.' Did you, really?" he asked.

I opened one eye again to see what his face looked like. Not good.

"I cannot believe you told your MOM!" I said, facing him and going for the offensive. I saw his mind track-switch immediately. Guilt is a wonderful thing.

"Alex, I swear I thought you would say something! What's your mom's schedule?"

I thought for a second—she'd left early, before I got up. She must be closing some deal.

"Well, she was gone early; maybe I have a bit of time, unless your mom catches her at work."

"I am *so* sorry," he said. The traffic in the hall was thinning and he realized he had to jet. "Look, I don't know what to say. I'm not a rat. I just was sure…."

I let it trail off, giving him a sort of nose-in-the-air, you-are-a-rat-but-I-am-trying-to-ignore-it look.

If my mom found out about the texts, I might never figure out where they were leading—or where they were coming from. And just as this Kiyosaki/cash flow thing was getting interesting.

Chapter Seven

On the bus home, I thought more about what my text angel had said. OK, so I know Charlie would give me that Look, but it just didn't feel like a stalker. And sure, I know that's exactly what the girl in the scream movie thinks as the music goes creepy and you can't help but shout at the screen, "TURN AROUND!" … but I wanted to roll with it, for a little while at least.

Until, yeah, fine, the evil scar-faced stalker takes me down with a chain saw from behind.

My angel had seemed to praise me for considering the Business angle. I couldn't read on the bus because it makes me carsick. But I could think—and text. I scrolled to the texts marked ALEX-MOBILE and wrote:

> re mlm what if i fail

The answer came back almost immediately:

> most do but whatf u dont

I had to smile at that. I'd done a little cybersurfing in the library before heading home; there was a lot out there about network marketing or MLMs, most of it bad. So bad, it hurt my head. I had no idea there were so many companies out there, and so many people determined to tell me that they had the product to make me millions of dollars with no effort. And tons of others to pick apart the 'losers' who believed in these 'scams.' There were dozens of juices, vitamins, internet portals, skin systems…did I mention my head hurt? I texted:

> K so wher 2 start

Maybe my text angel had some ideas. She—it freaked me out less to think she was a she—had pointed me at Kiyosaki. So maybe she had some ideas on what to do next. She didn't answer right away, and I dozed a little against the window. My stomach hurt because I kinda didn't want the ride to end. If Charlie's mom had reached mine, I could just imagine what was waiting for me when I got home. Just as the bus came around the big curve before my house, my phone pinged.

> if uv got kiyosaki def adler beach $

Huh? I was going to text back, but my stop was next. I gathered everything up and walked toward the front of the bus. As I spotted our driveway I saw two cars.

Both my parents were already home. Almost ran away right then.

I walked up the driveway, the text forgotten. I opened the back door quietly, trying to remain as silent as possible. I knew that they knew I was due home; the bus schedule was always the same, give or take. I resisted the temptation to do a whole CSI on their cars in the carport to find out how warm the hoods were; how long had they been home?

As soon as I got inside, I heard Dad's voice. My stomach did a flip. He was upset—really upset. They were obviously in the kitchen right on the other side of the door, at the table or by the stove. The door was closed. I crept up slowly.

"Olivia, I just don't know what we can do about this," he said, and his voice broke like Charlie's does sometimes. Mom was home too. I mean, I knew that from the cars, but both of them? Home?

Now? They must be talking about grounding me forever for not telling them.

"Tennessee!" I heard him say, and then it was muffled; all I could think was that Mom was hugging him.

What? Tennessee? I leaned forward, waiting to hear what came next.

The phone rang right next to me and I flinched. I moved back outside as silently as I could—I wanted to know what was going on, but I couldn't get caught spying. As I crept around to the kitchen window, I heard Mom pick up the phone, pause for a second, then say, "Beverly?" Her best friend. Charlie's mom. There was a little silence. I knew I was holding my breath when I started to feel dizzy, and slowly let it out through my nostrils while lowering my backpack off my aching shoulder. "Yeah, no, not the best time. Steve just found out… well, he found out that he's likely to be transferred," Mom said, and I felt my heart leap into my throat.

"He went in today, and they said that his whole division is moving to Tennessee," Mom said. "It has to do with that merger. It's going to take a while to get everything and everyone organized, but it's a done deal." Mom paused. "That's part of the problem," she said. "My license is only for here. I don't think I can waive into the Tennessee Bar—and besides," she said, sighing, "We don't have an office there, so if we go, I would need to get another job on top of passing another Bar."

Mom's voice was shaking. Mom. *My* mom. I was not at all used to hearing her sound so vulnerable. "So we have to figure this out," she said, and pulled her breath in with a quaver. "I suppose we could stay here until Alex is in college, with Steve commuting back when he can. Or we could all move," she said, and I drew in my breath, thinking *OMG no!*, "…but that would mean uprooting Alex in her Senior Year, new Bar exam for me, selling the house, all the rest. I don't know what we're going to do. I don't know at all. Right now we're, well, pretty devastated," Mom finished. Then, "But listen, you called me, what's up girl?" she said, obviously trying to add a little brightness to her voice. I winced. Here it comes. There was a silence. Then Mom said, "Oh, that's nice. Maybe I 'vibed' you with our issues. Thanks for just calling to see if everything was OK—you really are my best friend ever." I could actually hear a weak smile in Mom's voice.

Charlie's mom hadn't given me away—so, what now?

I had to head in there, but I wanted to give them some time. It took another couple of seconds before I figured the best way was to start over—loudly. I picked up my backpack in slo-mo so it wouldn't make a sound. Then I stomped up the back stairs, whacked open the screen, and noisily rattled my keys in the door lock.

"Hell-oooo-oooo!" I cried as soon as the door was open. "What are you guys doing home?" I asked because, well, their cars where both there and that was unusual. The kitchen door was closed, but I knew that. I heard some scurrying as I clomped towards the kitchen door like a truck driver. When I reached out to crack it open, Dad was gone—just Mom was there, making one quick swipe at her eyes as she took the kettle off the stove.

"Hey Alex," she said, in a brittle-bright voice. I noticed that her work clothes were still on, down to the shoes. Wow, this really was bad. There were six teabags in the garbage as I walked past it—they had been at this for a while. "Want some tea? How was school?" She turned away, and I knew that she was just saying something to say something. I wasn't sure what to do, so I sat down at the kitchen table—right on top of the stack of applications, which had made its way down to a chair this morning during breakfast. But I didn't dare move. Not so comfy—so be it.

I just sat there, watching her. She was rearranging things in the cabinets. Mom's a Virgo—when she gets stressed, she organizes.

I smiled at her—not time to be a pouty teenager.

"You should take your work stuff off, before you spill something," I said, not sure how that would go over. She nodded absently, and then headed slowly down the hall.

I wasn't sure where Dad was. I was left with a steaming mug of tea and the cat looking at me from his long stretch on the heat register under the table. I didn't want to start homework, because I was pretty sure some sort of 'talk' was coming. This was a big deal—I didn't want to be halfway into something when they came back. So I texted Stephanie about Dad, then turned my phone on vibrate. No sense making anyone mad that I was broadcasting what was up, but I had to get some ideas. And Stephanie was always full of ideas.

Stephanie. She and I couldn't be more different. Maybe that's why we liked each other so much. Stephanie has super curly hair, is roundly curvaceous, and super ballsy (ovaries-y?). She doesn't care what people think of her. She wants to run her dad's empire; her folks have a huge house and a pool, and she and her older sister can basically shop 'til they drop. It's a different sort of life, and it's fun to have her as my friend.

Although she's definitely not your athlete type, Stephanie's always up to something extracurricular. Whether it's trying to horn her way onto the cheerleading squad just by being the loudest, or taking some random exotic dance class, she'll try just about anything that will get her noticed. I'm more the 'behind the scenes' type. Steffie's grades aren't great, but everyone seems to think she'll be off to Stanford for sure. That's where her dad went, and there's no lack of funds in that family. She'll slap the popular guys on the butt, cat-call out windows—she's something else. I love being around it. Her personality drives Charlie nuts though.

I pulled out the Kiyosaki book while I was waiting. I could hear some muffled talking coming from Mom and Dad's bedroom. I had gotten caught up in the Kiyosaki book last night after getting the applications outlined with Mom. The whole E/S/B/I thing was interesting. I'd always thought of people who had lemonade stands or mowed lawns or whatever as entrepreneurs. Well, they were 'entrepreneurial,' in that they were trying to think up ways to make money, but in each case, they were just making money by their own labor. The whole deal was to try to make money that was not tied to your own labor—or, at least, not after a while. So I guess if you started mowing lawns, then got enough jobs that you hired other kids to mow the lawns for you, and then someone else to collect the money and all that jazz, being S-Self-employed could morph into a B-Business. As long as you had more coming in than going out, you had cash flow and as long as you weren't the one doing all the work, you had a business.

I wondered if there was something to this, especially now that Dad was faced with having to move to keep his job. I knew he liked his company and the products—but he really worked a lot, and it wasn't as if we were living up the hill in one of the McMansions or I was filling out private school applications. There was also stuff in the Kiyosaki book I never thought about—funding retirement, things like that. I know that Mom talked a lot about their 401k, which is supposed to be what they will retire on. But sounds like it used to be that companies would pay you after you retired—something called a pension. That you would work for the company and then the company would pay you afterwards. Now, you were on your own. And without some sort of B-Business or I-Investments giving you a stream of cash, you could literally outlive your money, or get kicked to the curb, which sounded like was happening to Dad. I was too young for this. But Kiyosaki pulled me in. It was so understandable, and for the first time I was thinking about what Mr. Sherman had been talking about in economics class. I was taking it because he was a nice person (for a teacher) and an easy grader, but now I was starting to think about what he put on the board.

Just by walking into our house this afternoon and hearing the anguished tone of Dad's voice—it was like walking out of a fog and into the hard light of reality. Where had I thought the money was coming from? Honestly, I hadn't thought about it much. My folks didn't want me to worry about stuff like that. I was totally doing the "E" thing. Expecting them to pay me my allowance for doing chores around the house on time, no questions, saving nothing, living to my next 'paycheck.'

This book was getting my attention.

Just as my phone vibrated, I saw Mom turn out of their bedroom and start down the hall. I wasn't sure what to do, but I knew for sure texting wasn't it. I had the Kiyosaki book out on the table as Mom came back into the kitchen. She was in her sweats, her hair back in a ponytail, but her makeup was still on. This was just so weird.

"Any homework I can help with?" she said in an absent-minded voice, heading for the freezer to get out some stuff for dinner.

"It's not so bad today—no worries," I said, and picked the Kiyosaki back up. I only had a few pages until the next chapter, and I thought I might be able to finish it before knuckling down and starting my homework.

Mom pulled out something microwavable, then took salad stuff out of the crisper. She looked at me, turned back, and then looked again, her eyes squinting a bit. "Is that Kiyosaki's book?" she said, with a hint of interest.

"Yeah, Dad loaned it to me yesterday."

"What do you think?" she said, setting spinach, tomatoes and feta on the counter. "Interesting?"

I was going to hit her with some of that great teenage silent glare stuff and a huff, sigh, and a "WHAT-ever…", just to be, well, a teenager, but at the last second I remembered what I'd come home to. "Believe it or not, yes," I said. "It makes me want to figure out how to be a B. I definitely get how you can get tied up being an E-employee or self-employed, and once you have debts, you're stuck. You said that you and Dad tried the whole I-investment thing, and then you tried a B-business—but it wound up being just 'time for money' or in other words, an S. I want to figure out how to start off right. And if I can figure out how to have a business, maybe I can wind up doing what I want in the end, not getting stuck in a job to pay off debts."

Mom actually stopped chopping tomatoes and looked at me, with a little glimmer in her eye. I don't think I'd said that many words to my mom in months. She definitely gets the brunt of my teen-aged-ness, which I suppose isn't fair, but she also always seems to be the one telling me what to do and what not to do. Not that I'm saying it's not right—I'm just saying that it sucks.

"That *is* interesting," she said. She stood there with the knife in one hand, half of a tomato in the other. "Are you actually serious?" she asked, focusing on me like a laser.

"Well…yes," I mumbled. I hadn't expected this. "Yeah, I think so, yeah." I closed the book on my finger, looking at her. It was odd. It was like we were just two people, not a mom and a daughter.

"Heeeeey!" I heard from the hall, and looked up to Dad in one of his surfer t-shirts, board shorts and tube socks. He didn't look that good—his nose was red and his eyes a little puffy. How could you let something like a job do that to you?

"Alex has an interesting idea," Mom said, turning to Dad, continuing before he could say anything. "She has been reading your Kiyosaki book, and said she wants to get started out right—

not as an employee or as a self-employed person, but having a business. I'm wondering whether that might be something we need to throw into the mix…you know." Dad squinted his eyes and pulled his chin in—he'd walked in on a conversation he hadn't expected.

"As in…?" he asked, cocking his head. The look that passed between Mom and Dad said a lot. "Hmmm," he finished, and turned on his tube-socked heel, heading back down the hall and into the study toward his library of books. Mom turned back to finish the salad and stick whatever was in the box in the microwave. I settled back down and opened the book off my finger, to finish the last couple of pages in the chapter before I had to set the dining room table for dinner. I could tell it was going to be another family dinner night.

Chapter Eight

Dinner was less than stellar at first. I was in this weird predicament. I knew what was coming, but I couldn't let them know I knew. It started with the whole, "So how was school today?" stuff, though I knew they were trying to figure out how to break the situation to me. Mom didn't even mention the college applications, though she's been on me about them every day for weeks. During one of the chewing-food-only silences, I figured it wouldn't hurt to backtrack to last night, when everything was happy and normalish. Man, only 24 hours …

"So, I've been reading the Kiyosaki book," I started, to see how that would play. Mom and Dad both nodded. I guess they wanted to see where this was going. OK, and me talking and us eating dinner was a new thing, too. Maybe they were just shocked a civil, conversational person had bodysnatched their daughter. I put down my fork and held my hands up, palm out, "Just hear me out, OK?" Now they were curious —Mom with an I'm-sure-I'm-not-going-to-like-this look, Dad with a this-could-be-interesting look that seemed to perk him up a bit.

I took a deep breath. "This is what I've been thinking. In the book, Kiyosaki compares his poor dad and his rich dad. His poor dad was all, 'Go to school, get a job, work for The Man.'" Mom took a bite of her salad, Dad nodded and looked thoughtfully down at his plate. "I get how that's just not so great. Look at what happened with your job," I said, and Dad's head jerked up before he realized I was talking to Mom. I ignored this reaction and continued, since I didn't want to let on I knew about his situation. "I wasn't that old, but I remember. It sucked. You did what you knew how to do; you started up your law firm That was pretty much the end of family vacations." Mom's face soured a little, so I hurried on. "I'm not complaining. I'm just saying, we'd go, then you'd be stuck in some condo or hotel room trying to deal with some client's emergency. Really, Dad and I were on vacation—you were just working in another location." Mom snorted a little. I could see she agreed. "So I get the E and the S thing. As an employee, you're stuck making what you make, trying to save a little to escape or retire. And from the sound of things, that's not easy. You also have to work where and when they want you to." Dad and Mom shared a glance, but I continued. "As an S, you're doing somewhat the same thing, maybe for what looks like more money and time freedom at first, but without the luxury of really knowing what's coming in your check every two weeks."

"How'd you get sooooo smart?" Dad asked with a smile in his eyes. I pointed at Mom, and for the first time during that meal the room felt a little less heavy.

"Anyway—I've been thinking. What if we were to do the B—a business? I can't face the idea of learning investing. Stocks, options, tax liens, it just sounds revolting." Mom ducked her head for a second to hide a smile. "And," here it comes, I thought, "If we got a business going, maybe I shouldn't go right to college."

I held up my hand again, palm out, as Mom about levitated in her seat. This was the part I knew they wouldn't like. "I'm just saying," I hurriedly continued, hand still out, "What if we had a business, like one of those MLMs, and worked on it for reals? If it works the way Kiyosaki says, there'd be cash flow, and that'd mean I could maybe go to college and study what I want, not what will get me a job. Hey, as a business owner, maybe I'd even learn about the subjects you want me to, because I could apply it. But either way, it's less of a sinkhole of money without any real goal in sight. Right? You know?"

Once again—probably the most I'd said to my parents in a year. And—they even seemed to be listening.

"I don't like the idea of you not applying to college, Alex," Mom turned to me. When I started to talk, she made my 'palms out' hand gesture right back at me, which I suppose was fair enough. I waited. "When I tried an MLM, it turned out to be pretty much a second job, not our path to financial freedom. And you'd be surprised how many people will just shut you down if you try to talk to them about it. Everyone 'knows someone who knows someone' who has wasted time or money on one. But that being said, I'm interested in this idea."

Dad nodded his head too; for the first time since I'd walked through that kitchen door this afternoon, he looked engaged.

"I have a proposition right back for you," she continued. "Some of the schools that we have applications for have an option that once you get in you can delay your acceptance. That means you're still admitted, but you can start with another class in the spring, or even next fall. What if you do a little research and see which schools have that option? We only apply to the ones with the option. Then," she said, gesturing to Dad with her head, her ponytail swaying, "you guys figure out if there's a way we can make a business while I keep doing my stuff and help where I can. The only deal though," she said, a warning in her voice, "is that this can't take over your worlds. Dad's going to be working; you're going to be going to school, homework, and the rest. This can come out of your other spare time—TV, mall-time with Stephanie, texting or Facebook-prowling. " She definitely knew me, I thought with a wince. "And no matter how excited you get, school has to come first."

She looked at Dad. He looked at her, then looked at me. He rolled his shoulders, reaching back behind the chair and clasping his hands together, pulling his arms back straight to stretch his back as he stood.

I looked at his half-eaten dinner—Dad never leaves food. But there was a light in his eyes again. "I think I'll take a poke at the Internet," he said, turning from the table. He took two steps, then looked back and grabbed his plate.

"Don't you get that in the keyboard!" Mom mock-sternly warned, though you could hear the smile in her voice.

Well, that hadn't gone badly.

"I think we'll pay for that University of Hawaii application after all," Mom said, looking sort of gratified at my astonished stare.

I dug into the rest of my salad. I had some research to do.

Chapter Nine

"I heard," Charlie said, sliding into the plastic seat across from me in the school cafeteria.

Charlie doesn't text—that means his mom had told him about dad's job situation because I knew I hadn't.

And maybe—ok think about it—maybe I didn't actually know yet. It hadn't come up. Dad had gone to the computer, I had done homework and started the research on which schools had the delayed admittance deal, Mom had taken over cleanup...and then bed and...no one told me anything. This was turning out to be some week.

"This is just so weird," I mumbled, blowing on my cup of decaf. The cafeteria's coffee is definitely not American's finest, but it's hot and cheap. People slammed trays on tables around us, frantically finished homework, or bopped to silent music playing only in their own ears.

"It's weird, you're right," he said, toying with the plastic cover I'd slipped off the top of my coffee. "I can't believe your dad might not be around. I would hate that. Sometimes I feel like we have the only intact families in America—but now...well, OK it's not divorce...it's *not*," he said, gesturing emphatically at my angry expression. "I know I know, the 'Big D'. Even I know that one in your and Steffie's code. But here you are, your dad is going to be off and away for weeks at a time. What about the little things he'll miss? Man being an adult is *not* easy."

Charlie knew my issue with the D-word. I'd been totally afraid, before Mom went back to a law firm, that my parents were on their way to the Big D, and he knew it. The stress had been intense; the energy in our house was always edgy and nasty. Definitely not a lot of family dinners back then.

"Actually, what I meant by it being weird is that they didn't even tell me last night." Charlie's eyebrows shot up, but I continued. "Long story, but as for the job thing, dad has a while to make up his mind," I said, taking another sip of the coffee. "If he moves, they'll move him—and us—or he can just keep going the way he is. But then he'll lose his chance to be farther up in management after the re-org. So if he says yes now he keeps his rank, but he goes to Tennessee. If he says no, then either he can leave now or stay until the end. He'll head up the transition teams and all that jazz, but at the end of the day he's out of the job." I knew I sounded bitter. "And after all those years, too. I can't believe it. Seriously? He's moved his way up, done the right things and been totally loyal. Look where that got him."

Charlie shook his head. He'd managed to fold the lid of my coffee cup cover, and was now tearing the edges into a little plastic flower.

"OK, so like I said—they didn't even tell me last night! We got going on this other thing, and so I'm not sure if I even know or not. My head hurts!"

Charlie pushed the 'flower' across the table and tilted back precariously on two thin plastic chair legs. "You don't know about that. They don't know about your stalker. What *were* you guys doing last night?"

Just as I started to elaborate, Stephanie came in the side door, shouting "A-lo-HA, Chica!" when she saw me. Stephanie was a bit much for Charlie. He rocked the chair forward and excused himself to go join some of his track buddies.

"So?" she said, smiling at Charlie as he left. She was oblivious to what he thought, and probably wouldn't care anyway. "You left me hanging. What's up?"

I'd turned off my phone last night, and after a little homework I'd fallen asleep reading Kiyosaki. I didn't turn it back on until this morning. Shock, I know. And typical of Steffie, about forty texts rolled in when I flicked the power on. I'd quickly hit her back— `2M2x IRL caf b4 1st`—"Too Much To Text, meet me In Real Life in the Cafeteria Before First Period," and here she was.

"My life is really odd these last few days," I began, realizing I hadn't told her anything.

"So what's up?" she repeated, then turned around to look at the cafeteria Specials board. "Just a 'sec," she said, heading off. Mocha time.

While I sat at the table guarding Steffie's purple-gem-and-rhinestone-embellished book bag and nursing my lukewarm coffee, I contemplated what was going on. And I thought *Hamlet* was complicated. I hadn't really remembered—until talking to Charlie—that Mom and Dad didn't know that I knew about Dad. I also hadn't told them about my text angel, which might send them into orbit. And Charlie's mom still held that ticking time bomb. I wondered whether Steffie could just ship me off to Hawaii for a month on her dad's American Express black card? I smiled a bit watching Steffie flirt her way to the front of the line.

"Hey!" A backpack crashed on the table—Josh from English. "What up!" He started to take the chair across from me, but noticed it was conspicuously occupied by Steffie's backpack.

"Do you ever think about college?" I asked looking up, my tone soft. He got a belligerent flare in his nostrils at first, but by my tone he knew I hadn't meant it as a cut. It was just a question.

"You know my mom's situation, Alex-zander-ah," he said, stretching out my name to make it sound weird. Yeah don't ask me why the Z, ask my dad. "I'll be lucky to be working for Mike's Tires after we blow this hell hole."

The thing that I knew—and it had taken Kelly, Miss Young's lackey and also a worker bee in the Records Office, to throw me this bone—was that Josh had a very high-B average. He liked to posture like he was Mr. Behind-The-Gym—but he was smart. I never let on that I knew, but it meant I could push him on this stuff.

"Serious, Josh. What are you going to do? You're not Mike's Tires material."

He thought for a second, and was just opening his mouth when Stephanie showed back up, a gigantic mocha in her hand.

"Josh!!!!" she said, and did a little hip-rocking happy dance. "How's hot man on campus?" Josh was definitely a cutie—blondish-brown wavy hair, broad shoulders, that whole bad boy look.

He smiled at her, flashed me a "V" sign and said "Peace, out."

"So!" After a long admiring glance as Josh left, Stephanie took the cap off her mocha blowing and talking while she was slurping. "Spill it. What is going ON!?" Her copper-flecked hazel eyes locked onto me.

"Oh Steffie, I don't even know where to start," I said. She took my nearly empty coffee cup and poured about a quarter of her gigantic mocha into it, never leaving the eye-lock.

"Yeeees?"

"So, I got home, and well, I have to tell you this other thing too. But so I got home and I heard Mom and Dad through the kitchen door talking about his work. He has to move to Tennessee to keep his job, or be part of a stay-team and then lose his job, basically." She waved her hand over the mocha to cool it, grimacing.

"O-M-G!"

"Yeah. The thing is that they didn't even talk to me about it last night. They—well...I have to backtrack. I have this text angel, and I got reading this book that Dad had, and so I..."

Stephanie actually blinked.

"You have a what?" she said quietly. I'd caught her off guard.

"I, well, I have this stalker, but I don't really think so. I think I have an angel who is contacting me using my phone."

I pulled out my cell, to show her. "See?" I asked, scrolling through, "It's from me somehow. ALEX-MOBILE. I thought I was being pranked, but the texts keep answering or talking about what's going on with me. It's got to be... it's gotta be an angel," I finished, a little lamely.

She read the texts—no Charlie problem there. Unlike him, Steffie is "text fluent." She pursed her lips. "B/I and E/S?" she said.

"Long story—but that's what got me talking to Dad, and turns out the whole Kiyosaki thing is for reals and ties into that."

Stephanie thought for a moment, rolling the phone in her hands. "You sure this isn't some like bugged phone thing?" she offered, but I shook my head.

"I wasn't on the phone, Steffie. I think it's...I think it's a text angel."

"And your parents...?" she said, just as the buzzer sounded for first period. She slid my phone back to me as we gathered up our stuff. I took a long sip to finish the mocha that Steffie had deposited in my cup, then pitched the cup into a bin.

"Yeah, that's the thing," I said, shrugging my shoulders. "My folks don't know about that. And I don't know about Dad's job. It's a mess." I felt a little odd then realized—Steffie always has triple espresso.

"Dang girl," I said as we parted for separate classes, "I'm going to have a sugar-caffeine meltdown by the end of class!"

"That's how you know it's time for another!," Steffie said, laughing as the crush of students carried her away.

Chapter Ten

Back home that night things were back to normal. Both Mom and Dad were working late, so I fixed myself something out of the freezer and took it down to my room. Mom hates this—I'm supposed to make a salad, sit at the table—but it's such a pain to do for just me.

I spread a bath towel out on the far side of my bed and put the microwaved dinner on top of it. Then I lay down and pulled the towel up over my side. No sense getting what I was eating either all over the bedspread or all over me, as ultimately I'd have to pay for it when I had to do my wash. I booted up my computer on my stomach, typing with my right hand and mindlessly forking dinner in with my left. It was some spring pasta prima-something, but it just tasted like red sauce.

I hadn't had the chance to research the last directive from my text angel. She said that if I had read Kiyosaki, then "def"–definitely–"adler beach $" was next. I didn't know what she meant, but this time, I decided to put "adler beach $" into Google. If I had done that with Kiyosaki, I would have gotten the *Rich Dad* thing without having to call Dad—but then again, calling Dad had started stuff rolling. This time, I'd see what I could find by myself.

The search pulled up some listings for Adler Beach, but in between there were reviews for a book called *Beach Money* by Jordan Adler. That sounded like it. There were also a couple YouTube videos.

I started watching my way through the videos, and I got intrigued. It was what Mom and Dad had been talking about—network marketing. This guy seemed to be some sort of a guru, like Kiyosaki, but he looked less like a suit and more like a regular guy. I was intrigued. Though it looked like Adler was involved with one specific company, people in all sorts of network marketing organizations cited his book.

When I went to the website for the book, the first thing that I heard was the crashing of waves on a beach. Then I saw that it promised to help show me how to live my dream life today, and how to turn the amount that someone earned yearly into their monthly income. The book was on the home page, with a guy that looked like him. He was sitting on a beach with a computer in front of him, his hands behind his head. I figured I'd tell Dad I'd found this website and see if he'd put the book on his credit card. Meanwhile, I started reading everything I could find.

The next thing I knew—but it must have been quite a while later since my room was totally dark—I heard the back door slam and my mom's heels striding across the kitchen floor. "Alexzandra!" she called, and I cringed. I quickly wrapped the towel around the empty plate and fork, stashing them under my bed, and not a moment too soon. Mom pushed my half-open bedroom door so hard it slammed on the wall.

"*What* is this about a *stalker*?" she said, and I could feel her eyes blazing at me until she flicked on the overhead light—then I saw them, too.

I sat up fast, nearly dumping my computer on the floor. Obviously, Charlie's mom had caught up with mine.

"It was a *prank*, Mom," I shot back. "And what about Dad getting *fired*?" I said, matching her accusatory tone. "That grapevine goes two ways, Olivia," I said, using her first name, which she hates me to do…and I know it. Hey, the best defense is always an offense—if you have one. She's the one who taught me that.

"He is *not* getting fired," she declared, but her tone wasn't quite so harsh. "And what do you mean, 'a prank'?" She crossed her arms, waiting.

"It's a text-prank thing. Of course Charlie isn't Mr. Text, so he didn't know either. It's *so* not a big deal," I said, giving her the teenage-daughter glare. Of course, it's 'so no big deal' until my 'angel' turns out to be freakin' Mr. Chainsaw, but I didn't mention that.

"And so what about Dad?" I said, my voice lifting accusingly. I knew what was going on there, but I am definitely not above pressing the offensive if given the opportunity. Like mother, like…

"Yeah, well *that's* not a prank." Mom sighed and uncrossed her arms. She leaned against the wall next to my dresser. "Your dad found out that his whole division is being moved out of state. He has the opportunity to go, but of course that means relocating us, too. He doesn't want to do that, and neither do I. So he can stay and be the transition person—basically turning the lights out at the end. Or he can decide later, but if he does that, it's likely someone else will take his job—in Tennessee."

"That sucks," I said, because it did. "He's worked there pretty much his whole life."

"I know honey," Mom said, "But I have to tell you, what you said last night actually changed Dad's calculus a little." She threw a small smile at me. "I think we were pretty much resigned to him moving as soon as possible—so he wouldn't lose his upward mobility—and then commuting back when he could. There's no way we were going to pull you out of school and frankly, it would be a pain for me too, considering I am just starting to get my own book of business at the firm." I hadn't thought about that. Mom had gone back to the firm after being in-house for years and then having her own practice for a while—so though she was older, it was almost as if she was a new partner. To build up business, plus having to take another state's bar exam so many years after she'd gotten her license…yeah. That did not sound like fun times.

"I have been doing a little research, actually," I said, and when she raised her eyebrows, I added, "After homework, swear." She smirked and I continued. "I think I might want to get a book. It's called *Beach Money*. Do you happen to have that one in the study?" She shook her head. I didn't tell her, of course, that I'd gotten a little help in finding that title; instead, I said, "It's a book that easily explains network marketing, and it's mentioned by a lot of people who work a lot of different network marketing businesses. It's not just one company saying it. And they all say it's a really good book to read—a great overview."

The sides of Mom's mouth turned down while her brow furrowed thoughtfully. "Hmmm. I actually have to get changed and Dad isn't coming home until later. They have a transition team meeting tonight, and he doesn't want to miss anything—just in case we decide he has to go to Tennessee," she said. "Why don't you email us the information, so that we can check it out?" She turned to head out of my room, but stopped short. "You're really sure that this isn't a real stalker? Charlie was worried, so of course Beverly is worried, which made me very worried."

"I'm sure," I said, trying to sound sure.

"As long as you know you can tell us anytime if it becomes a problem. Did you eat?" she said, and I nodded, avoiding the urge to sneak a glance toward the towel-wrapped bundle under my bed.

Mom headed out, and I opened my computer and booted up email, to cut and paste them the information on the Adler book. Then I thought I'd head over to Twitter for a few, just to see what everyone else was up to. Hey, I'm a teenager. Don't hate.

Chapter Eleven

"...so, that's where it's at." Stephanie was foaming the milk onto her cappuccino as I finished my tale of last night's events. She put both our drinks on a tray with a plate of biscotti, and carried them to the bright kitchen table overlooking their pool through a floor-to-ceiling window.

Her folks have this amazing home—just the kitchen is beyond belief. Our living room could fit in here, no problem. Stephanie already knew her way around their new gigantic Italian espresso machine with all the bells and whistles—her dad's latest gadget. I accepted the red Stanford Alum mug of decaf Americano and one of the cookies.

"Steffie, I swear, how many shots of espresso are in that thing?" I asked, glancing over at what looked more like a bowl of cappuccino sitting in front of her.

"Just enough," she replied coyly.

Earlier, Mom had agreed that Stephanie could drive me home from school so long as we did our homework, but we had mainly been talking about my text angel, what I'd learned about network marketing, and of course—it being Stephanie—boys.

"I want to see the text angel thing happen with my own eyes," she continued.

"I'm not sure that she—or he—will appear on cue," I said warily.

In fact, I'd been very careful about how many texts I'd even sent to my angel—it felt like any second, I could just get a "C Ya" and that'd be that. In the meantime, Dad had ordered *Beach Money*, as well as a few others he'd seen online. He was even checking out various companies, then reporting back to Mom—letting her play 'devil's advocate' about the opportunity proposition on each. Sometimes, if I was around, they'd call me into the living room. We'd each lie on one of the couches and dream about what we'd do in a few years if this got up and running. Tazo Tea was making bank on our family; mugs and mugs of tea could be involved if we really got going. Being Mom, Mom made rules, of course; no one got to poke fun at the others and everyone had to be supportive. Dad had read that this was the most important step—to really get a picture of why you were doing this. Apparently, at the beginning there would be more work than cash, and you had to just keep at it until you got to a 'tipping point,' which could take a while. So you had to have a concrete prize you could see—with all your five senses—and keep your eye on that prize during the ramp-up time.

I learned a lot about my folks. Dad wanted to teach surfing—no surprise there. But Mom wanted to learn how. Seriously? We both wanted to go and work at Best Friends Animal Sanctuary. And Mom also wanted to teach kids like me, and even older folks like them, about the B-Business stuff. Teach? Mom? Then again—why not? I realized that, while Mom's a great lawyer, I think she's tired of it. Even though she doesn't go to court—she deals with negotiations and contracts—she says that someone always had to give, someone always got to take. I think she wants to have some fun, not think so hard, have a win/win.

OK, so, I don't think I ever really thought of my folks as real people. I never had thought about their hopes and their dreams. And I felt they were treating me like a real person, not a kid, too.

"Try it. Text her." Stephanie's voice brought me out of my reverie. I pulled my phone out of my back pocket, looking at her skeptically. Steffie was quick—she had it out of my hands before I could blink.

"Hey!" I said, trying to get my phone back. She went right to that string of texts, typed fast, and pressed Send. Then she flipped the phone back onto the table, looking smug.

I didn't even want to look. The silence was deafening.

"Your phone is so blah," she finally said coyly, eying it, then spinning it on the table. She knew I wanted to grab it, and I knew she knew, so I tried to act cool, sipping my decaf. "We have to bling it out more."

Stephanie's phone was rhinestone-embellished, just like her book bag… and anything else she could get her hot glue gun on. Not exactly my thing. Last month I'd let her add a line of black stones to the back of my phone, and one rhinestone at the top—that was the extent I'd let that glue gun near me.

The phone buzzed.

We both looked at it. Uncharacteristically, her voice was hushed. "You get it," she whispered, pushing the phone in front of me.

I picked it up, trying to look nonchalant. But my hands were icy cold as I tapped in the security code.

> whatf i dont blv in u steffie we even?

I burst out laughing, scanning the preceding text—the text that Stephanie had obviously sent.

> yo txt angel whatf i dont blv in u

I handed the phone over to Stephanie, who read it—and yipped. I remember that reaction—of course, last time it had come out of my mouth!

"How did you *do* that?" she said accusingly. I held up my hands, palms forward. I suddenly realized that, though she'd read the text string when we were in the cafeteria, seeing it 'in action' was different. Stephanie is all about control, and this was something that she couldn't even pretend she could understand. Like, how'd the angel know the text was from her? Steffie thought I knew. Nope. She gulped down the rest of her cappuccino, heading back to the Gaggia for more.

"Girl, no more coffee," I said. "See what I've been dealing with?"

She stopped mid-step, turned back around, took one step back toward the table, then turned back toward the espresso machine, then back toward the table, undecided. That was a first. Stephanie, undecided and speechless? Never.

"Do you think that it can give us answers to tests? Or stock picks? I mean…" Stephanie's voice trailed off.

I shook my head. "I'm not even going to ask," I said firmly. "I don't know where she or he is coming from, but remember the movie where the girl loses those powers 'cos she starts using them for money? I don't want to be like that." OK, sure, I was quoting from a late night movie as if it was fact. But where would *you* go to find anything to compare…?

"I ask questions, but I try to stay in line with where this all started," I continued. "And if you think about it, I don't even really know *how* it started. In fact, I keep wondering if I got into some sort of crossed circuits. The first text was like she was listening to Charlie and me. I don't know. But either way, I'm not going to go all *Back To The Future* with this," I finished, citing an '80s movie Steffie and I had channel surfed into when I was spending the night last summer. "If anything, that's for sure asking for trouble."

"So, what next?" she said, and I shrugged. She shook her head, staring at the phone warily.

I leaned back, watching out the floor-to-ceiling window as their gardener raked the polished river stones next to the pool. "I don't want to be a bother, which sounds stupid enough already."

"You crack me up, Alex," she said, toying with the piece of chocolate-dipped biscotti in front of her. "I never would've thought that. I'd be texting all day, asking this and that, and you think about bothering them? Send her one more," she pressed, and I gave her the stink eye.

"We have to get our homework done," I said, pulling out my books and dropping them in a heap on the table.

"One," she pleaded. This was going nowhere. I couldn't just leave, either. Stephanie had given me a ride from school in her 16th birthday present red Mercedes Roadster, so I was her hostage—I couldn't just walk home.

I thought for a minute. I really didn't want to tick my angel off, but Stephanie would pester me until I did something…and we wouldn't get homework done until then either. I opened up my phone.

JC WU@

Not exactly asking for the keys to the kingdom, but where my text angel was located was definitely something I'd been "JC"—Just Curious—about for a while. I showed Stephanie, and she shrugged her shoulders.

"Not a very sexy question," she said, to which I stuck out my lower lip. "Yeah, but I wonder where she's at, too. Maybe…?" Stephanie let her phrase dangle, pointed up at the ceiling, and raised her eyes and eyebrows in question.

"Where? You think she's upstairs in your parents' bedroom?" I deadpanned, and she snorted, just as the phone buzzed back. We both stared at it. I figured I'd be magnanimous, and flicked my fingers at the phone in a 'Go Ahead' gesture.

Stephanie grabbed it, but didn't look at the text right away. "You know you're using our shorthand, right?" she said. I nodded. I guess Steffie had just realized that *all* the texts were in our shorthand, from the first. We nearly bonked heads as we leaned in to read the message simultaneously.

-h8 lml n loha ttfn

Stephanie had made up "lml"—*Livin' My Life*—as a way to indicate being happy, and in an awesome state of mind. "-h8" had been mine—"*No Hate*" or "*Don't Hate Me.*" So the whole text indicated, before the "ttfn" (all Tigger, dat), that my angel was happy, free, and in an awesome state, "livin' her life" in Hawaii (loha—for "*aloha*").

Steffie scrolled back through the conversation, then laughed. "Dang girl, your angel is living *your* life!"

I didn't get home until much later than I'd intended. I'd called to get the parental OK to stay for dinner—which translates as Stephanie and me eating almond butter off spoons and doing a bit of homework in between talking about my angel. My stomach hurt from all the coffee, too, even though I'd stuck to decaf. Not smart trying to keep up with Steffie's consumption rate. Mom and Dad were talking in the den when I got home.

"Come on in here, Alex," Dad said when they heard me walking by. They both had smiles when I opened the door. "We've got something for you," he said, holding out the *Beach Money* book. I grabbed it and looked over the cover.

"Listen, your mom and I had an idea." Dad had tucked one foot up and under his other leg as he sat on the couch—a pose that, for the life of me, I couldn't figure out how he did without his leg going to sleep. I raised my eyebrows and he continued. "We've been going through a lot of the network marketing companies—there are so many more than when your mom was doing one before. We've kind of narrowed it down, and are trying to figure out the best way to approach this. There are plusses and minuses with a whole bunch of them. We want one that's been around long enough, but not so long that the market's saturated, where there isn't any scandal attached, that seems to have a good compensation plan and appeals to a wide range of people." He pointed at the book. "This Adler guy's company does seminars across the country—actually, even internationally. Your mother pointed out that there's one coming to the city next month."

I felt a rush in my chest—holy cow, things were really moving along.

"If I learned one thing from my last network marketing experience," said Mom, "it's that I want to have a good upline. Last time I liked the product so much, I just called the company and they assigned me a sponsor who didn't work with me. I didn't realize then that team building was the key. This time, I want to pick someone who is really serious, and who understands where we want to go and can help us get there, fast." I nodded. "So, when we saw that this author Jordan Adler was going to be in the city, we thought we'd go, and see what it's like—all three of us, of course," she added.

"Will they let us go?" I asked, wondering if you already had to have joined the company to go to their event.

"I'm sure they will. Now get some sleep," Dad said. "This is going to start getting interesting."

Chapter Twelve

The time flew by between our 'family decision' to check out the *Beach Money* ™ guy's MLM and the seminar in the city. Dad and I finished his book. It's like I had the key to open up a world I had never even known existed.

I tried to bring up some of what I was learning to friends. They generally said it sounded like a con game, but despite their reservations some were still curious. Dad had some other books in the study that I started reading also, by guys like Og Mandino and Richard Bliss Brooke.

Charlie told me that his Mom supported mine to her face, but apparently was of the opinion that mom would wind up with a bunch of products in the closet again, really just being, as Kiyosaki would put it, an "S". I actually even obliquely mentioned it to my guidance counselor, Mrs. Mellici, when she asked why I'd only applied to some of the schools on my list. From the look on her face, I could just see her calling my parents to tell them how foolish they were being. That did make me smile though. Mom versus Mrs. Mellici. Heya. Heya. Step Right Up.

The more I read, the more excited I got about the seminar. When the day finally came and we were driving to the city though, the car actually felt a little tense. We all didn't know what to expect. Mom had called the company and they said that no one was turned away. We could just show up. So that's what we were doing.

We listened to one of Dad's Automobile University talks. This one was Zig Ziglar. He's hilarious in a low-key, countryish way. Dad picks CDs like these up from the library, loads them on his MP3, and then has them to listen to when he's driving.

Ziglar's talk was common sense, but profound at the same time. Ziglar would get you laughing at his goofy stories and examples, which helped people remember them…smart. One of his big points was that the first thing before you started on a new path was truly believing that what you wanted was possible. If you didn't believe in yourself, people would smell that the way a Doberman smells fear. Made sense to me.

After driving a couple hours and a healthy dose of Automobile University, Dad pulled up in front of the venue. Once inside, we saw a mob scene in front of a registration table. Dad and I hung back while Mom waded in to sign up. When she came back with our guest badges, she gave us an excited smile.

"Now remember, we split up at breaks and talk to as many people as we can, then we'll compare notes later." Mom edged us closer to the closed auditorium doors. "If we're going to be serious, we're going to sign on with someone who is serious, too. I believe in us, and we need a person who will work just as hard as we will to get us where we want to go. We need to learn fast, but we also need to know that we won't be left behind. I didn't know a lot about direct marketing when I first got into it last time, but I know more now. And I know the sort of person that we need."

When we couldn't get any closer to the doors, she pushed me forward a little.

"Here's your first task," she said. "Get up there. Be nice, but keep moving until you're right up to the doors. You're young and friendly. They're going to be enchanted by you; they'll ask why you're here—all that jazz. Once you get to the doors, stay there. When the doors open, I want you to get right up as close to the front as you can and hold three seats. The really serious people are going to be up in the front rows."

I had my marching orders. So I channeled the way Stephanie always 'works it' to get to the front of the line at the cafeteria. As I wormed my way forward I talked a little, laughed, smiled, made some small talk, and motioned back to my folks when I had to. They'd politely wave. I figured that people saw my guest badge and thought that Mom and Dad were already part of the company and had just brought me along. I also realized that's exactly what Mom was hoping for.

As soon as the doors opened, people rushed forward. I swayed but stayed on my feet, and headed up to the front seats. Music was pumping, and a man on the stage cheerfully welcomed everyone into the room. I'd never seen anything like it. Everyone seemed really happy, laughing and hugging each other—probably seeing folks they hadn't seen for a while, I thought.

I was able to grab three seats in the third row—the front two rows were already taken. I couldn't figure out how, since I was among the first people to enter the room. Then it occurred to me—this is what Mom meant. Those people knew people. They had reserved their seats somehow. These must be the people we wanted to know.

Mom and Dad caught up to me just as I saw Jordan Adler. He was over to the side, chatting with some other folks who also might be presenters. He looked just like on his book, pretty relaxed and friendly. It was a little hard to believe that he was a Distributor just like everyone else. He didn't own the company, he just worked the system like anyone could.

"Why don't we ask Mr. Adler to sponsor us?" I asked Mom loudly over the music, gesturing to where he stood. Other people had seen him by that time, and were having their pictures taken with him. She nodded, as if thinking about the question.

"I thought about that," she said back, talking right into my ear to be heard. "We should look into that, but we should also consider other Distributors. We want an upline who will give us their attention right away. I keep thinking of Goldilocks," she continued, smiling. "We don't want a sponsor who's got an enormous team already, we don't want a sponsor who doesn't know what they're doing; we want one who will be…" and I joined her in the phrase from the old nursery book, "Just Right."

That made sense—if Mr. Adler was giving big presentations internationally, working his business, being pulled aside for photos, and stuff like that—it wasn't like someone who only had a hundred or so people on their team. As I understood it from some of the folks I had talked to in line, Mr. Adler had thousands and thousands on his team. Wild.

The music pumped up even more, if that was even possible. The M.C. on stage worked the audience. When he announced Mr. Adler, the place erupted. Everyone was standing, cheering and clapping their hands over their heads to the music. Whew—this was nuts. I looked at Mom, who smiled at me, then reached over and squeezed my hand.

"This stuff is always crazy," she shouted over the rumbling bass note of the music, "But it's fun, too. Just get a load of how crazy a bunch of adults can get, and remember that everyone is here for the same reason we are—to learn something that will help them build their businesses."

Mr. Adler stepped up to the mike, and I joined in with the clapping. I'm not sure what I'd expected—something more like a lecture, I guess. Definitely not music, stomping feet, and wild energy. This was unchained.

At the break, we worked our strategy and split up, each of us talking to someone different. It reminded me of when Charlie's family would go Christmas tree shopping—everyone would fan out, looking for The Tree, then mark the spot and head back to compare, to ultimately get the 'best' one. Mom said, if possible, to try to stay near and talk to the front row people. Always the lawyer, she wanted us to note if their attention strayed when talked to, what they asked, and how relaxed they made us feel.

It was a little hard to hear, since they played the music during the break, too. What was interesting to me was that Mr. Adler had gotten up on the stage, but mainly he was introducing another person—the founder of the company—who was going to be the main presenter. They obviously knew each other well, but then Mr. Adler sat down right in the front row, to hear what was said, just like the rest of us. Here's this guy who makes more each month than most people made in a year, but he was there to learn just like we were.

I watched Dad start talking to the older woman who had sat right in front of us, as Mom approached a young couple that was over to the left side in the front row. Though I knew I was supposed to pick someone, I decided to head out of the room. There was just no way I could talk over the music, and I certainly couldn't hear that well. I caught Mom's eye and signaled to her where I was heading, and she gave me a thumb's up. Just as I turned to head out, a woman from the row in front of me stepped out into the aisle and we ran right into each other.

She laughed, stepping back. "Are you OK?" Her round cinnamon face broke into a bright smile. She asked the question looking me right in the eyes, one of the things Mom had mentioned to us in the car ride down.

"I'm good," I said. "Actually, I think I hit you harder. Are you OK?"

She laughed, bending her neck from side to side. "Just a touch of whiplash—you have insurance, right?" she kidded. Unlike some of the people I'd met so far, she wasn't treating me like a child.

We headed up the aisle and through the door, away from the music and hubbub. "Where are you from?" she asked once we were outside. Again, I could see she was really looking at me, not through me.

I told her. "I've always wanted to visit up there," she said. "I actually flew in, myself—I'm just here for a couple days though." I must have looked puzzled, so she continued. "A lot of us go to these even if they're not in our towns—the thing I like best about this company is that they don't sit you down for hours to push product or consider everyone as having a fifty dollar bill on their forehead ready for you to pluck off. I actually heard that from another company I was in before. Here, it's all about personal development. Every time I go to one of these, I learn something new—usually about myself."

I thought about what we'd heard so far. It was a little like the Ziglar guy we'd listened to in the car. If you ask me, it was way better than I'd expected. Not only was I starting to believe we could do this, but I could see that Mom was excited, too. And even though I hadn't been able to see Dad, because he was on the other side of Mom, I'd noticed he wasn't getting fidgety, which happens a lot when he gets bored.

"I'm Sophie," she said suddenly, as if just remembering we hadn't formally met yet. She put out her hand.

"I'm Alex," I said, and we shook hands formally but then both laughed at it. She had a nice smile, and shook my hand firmly.

"Are you here alone?"

I liked that—she didn't presume. "I'm here with my mom and dad."

"Are you guys with the company?"

"No, we actually came to check it out."

"Really?" she said, puzzled. "How'd you decide to come here?"

I figured it best to skip the text angel part. "A friend actually pointed me to a book by a Mr. Kiyosaki and then the one by Mr. Adler—so we decided to check out what Mr. Adler did since there are so many choices when it comes to network marketing companies."

"Oh, that's great. Yeah—the *Rich Dad* books—I love those. They actually gave me my start too, believe it or not. Made me see things differently." She paused and smiled as someone gave her a friendly pat on her shoulder in passing, then turned back to me. "So you came because of Jordan? So what do you guys think so far?"

I liked that—"you guys"—she assumed my family was a team. Most of the people I had talked to while working my way to the front of the line had asked if "they"—my parents—were with the company, not all of us. It made me feel invisible, but not here with Sophie.

"So far, it seems pretty cool."

"Well, since I know you came here because of Jordan, shouldn't you meet him? I'll check if he is still up at the front when we go back in, and I'd be happy to introduce you." Sophie smiled again, then hustled off to catch up with a friend before I even had the chance to snap out of my stunned silence. Meet Mr. Adler? Really?

A few other folks came up to talk with me—mainly people that I'd talked to in line. They were nice, but after a couple seconds would see someone they knew over my shoulder, and drift away. A few people handed me their card "for my parents," since they'd seen they were Guests from our stand-out fluorescent green badges. Some told me that when they—my parents—wanted to get started, they should call the number on the business card I was given, and they'd be well taken care of. "They" – not "me." Not "us." Though I took the cards, I wondered how in heck these people could imagine my folks would want to call them, when they didn't even know anything about us?

I was talking with an older guy when Sophie walked back up. He was telling me how he had lost everything, but how great this opportunity was and how he wished he'd known about it when he was my age. Sophie waited patiently and didn't interrupt—she smiled at him but ultimately he handed me a card and said to "keep him in mind."

"Ready?" she said brightly, and we walked back into the music and loud, good-natured chaos. We headed back toward our seats. Mr. Adler was there, so Sophie motioned to me and we walked up, waiting patiently as the people in front of us finished. A couple butted in front of us to get their copy of *Beach Money* signed; Mr. Adler looked up as he signed it, smiled at Sophie, and nodded slightly. I turned around as we were waiting, and spotted Mom and Dad, just as they saw me. I motioned for them to come up, and they started to weave their way through the people laughing and talking.

"Sophie!" Mr. Adler said, and then smiled at me expectantly.

"This is Alex," Sophie said, and Mr. Adler shook my hand. "She read your book, and it prompted her family to come and check us out."

"Nice to meet you Alex," he said, smiling into my eyes. He then looked up and behind me—I looked back. My parents had just walked up.

"Mr. Adler, this is my mom and dad, Olivia and Steve, Mom and Dad, this is Mr. Adler."

He smiled. "Jordan, please," he said to me in a mock stern voice, and then shook Mom's hand and said, "Olivia," and "Steve" as he shook Dad's, and Dad said, "Pleased to meet you, Jordan."

"You're all three Sophie's guests?" he continued.

Mom answered him. "No. Actually, Steve and Alex read your book. We're looking for a business opportunity, and when we went to your website we saw you'd be here, so we thought we might as well check out the company you're with." Mom smiled. "I particularly liked a part of your book Steve told me about," she said, gesturing to Dad, "Where you talked about the network marketing companies where you hadn't made it before—I know the feeling."

Jordan nodded and smiled. We were getting crowded from behind—he was a hot commodity. It was also almost time to take our seats again.

"Tell you what," Sophie said, "why don't you guys take a picture with Jordan? I'll send it to you and you can put it with your copy of *Beach Money*." Her dark brown eyes twinkled as she smiled, holding up her cell phone and stepping back. She moved her hands to indicate for us to squish into the frame. "Say 'Beach Money'!" she said, which made us all laugh. Then we thanked Mr. Adler, and moved away from the crush of people trying to get to him.

Sophie turned and asked, "Would you mind if I got your info? I'd really like to get this photo to you." I looked at Mom and Dad, and they nodded.

After I'd given her "I enjoyed meeting you, Alex," she said. "I wish I'd known about companies like this when I was your age. I'm not sure if you or your folks are going to have any questions, but I'd be happy to answer any if you like." She handed me her card, looking me right in the eyes. "No matter who you choose to sign up with, I really would like to keep in touch." As the M.C.'s loud bass voice repeated through the music that it was time for us to take our seats, she slipped into the row right in front of us, smiling at Mom and Dad before taking out her notebook.

I was glad I'd crashed into her. Or vice versa.

Chapter Thirteen

The day after the event, we were all still exhausted. Dad got up and made us his 'patented' chocolate chip and banana pancakes (no banana for Mom), and we had breakfast at the dining room table in our robes and slippers.

We hadn't discussed that much on the ride home—I think we were all a little overloaded. But at breakfast, per Mom's instructions, we sat down with our notebooks and the business cards we had collected.

As Dad put down a plate of pancakes at each place, Mom came in with juice, and I rounded it all up with butter and maple syrup. Mom went back and got the Thermos of coffee and put it on a trivet on the table, then surveyed our 'information piles.' Dad had a few bent-up business cards and then a few pages of notes. He must have taken paper from Mom's notebook; one edge was still furred where she had pulled the pages out of the spiral binding. In contrast, Mom had her notebook, and I could see she had already highlighted parts, with notes in the margins. The business cards she'd collected were perfectly straight. I was a mix of the two—bent up business cards, but copious notes in my own notepad.

"So, what do we think?" she started, as she cut into the steaming pancakes and smeared butter on a bite.

Dad chewed thoughtfully then said, "You know, I really liked the company. I can see that they have a good support system, which you said we should look for. I'm happy to go with this one.

Everything we've researched on them seems solid. The offering is easy to understand, everyone can use it, it serves a need, and costs less than retail. And the people seemed fun and enthusiastic."

"Of course, most people who go to things like that are," Mom warned, but Dad waggled his knife at her.

"I know," he said, swallowing a big bite of pancake. "But it didn't seem like empty rah-rah stuff. I learned a lot. It reminds me of when we would go to those Tony Robbins seminars way back when." Mom smiled and pointed to her chin, a signal to Dad he had a big smear of chocolate there. He wiped it off with his napkin and reached for his OJ.

"What about you, Alexzandra?" Dad asked.

"I was surprised," I said, as I picked at a melted chocolate chip on my top golden pancake. "I thought it would be like a lecture or school, but this was almost like a rock concert." Both Mom and Dad laughed. I paused, wondering if I should say what I was really thinking. They actually waited. "OK, so another thing that I liked is I got treated as an actual person by a lot of the people there, too, not just as a kid," I said. "Yeah, well so except maybe by this guy," I finished, holding up one of the business cards I'd been told to "give to my parents" and wrinkling my nose.

Mom looked like she was going to protest, but Dad interrupted. "I think I see what you mean," he said. "I hadn't thought of that, but it's a good point. You mean someone interacting with you and treating you seriously—not just as being 'with us.' It's like the old adage that you want to see how someone treats the elderly, dogs, and babies, to see who they really are. Not that you're a baby, of course," he smiled. "Or a beagle."

I snorted then laughed. "Daaad…."

Mom cut in, nodding her head. "Yeah OK I hadn't thought of that either," she said. "I did notice that sometimes we would be talking to someone, but they would only talk to me or your dad if we were there together."

"I could see Alex was getting steamed," Dad said, as I rolled my eyes—I hated being treated like an Invisible Girl. Mom plucked the business card from my fingers, smiled a slightly evil smile, crumpled it and threw it on the floor as I laughed out loud. "So," Dad continued, playing mindlessly with one of the other business cards in front of him, "What do we do now?" he gestured at the table. "Call all these folks? Compare who we liked and why?"

Mom smiled enigmatically and took a sip of her juice before speaking. "Actually, no," she said mysteriously. We looked up, puzzled. "Now, we wait to see who contacts *us*."

And so—we waited. Mom had come up with a whole strategy. Some of the folks that we had cards for didn't contact us at all. Heck, some had said to "call them" for more info on this "great opportunity"—and not asked for our info back! We could weed those business cards out in the first few days; they went into the "circular file" as my dad called the trash can.

Dad had set us up with special contact information before we'd headed out to the event. He'd gone to a private mailbox place and gotten us a box there. He'd also set us up with a separate email and Google Voice account. He'd even done up some calling cards for each of us on the Dream Choosers Team as we were calling ourselves. It had been kinda fun having my own card, and boy was I surprised at how many people asked for it! Dad said that this way, especially with the private mailbox and such, no one had our "real" information—cell phone numbers, address, emails—which freaked him out a little, especially for "his girls."

I'd asked about the private mailbox, which was now my responsibility to check on the way home from school, instead of just one at the post office. Dad explained that if you got one through the post office your address was P.O. Box. This way, our cards actually had a street address and a suite number instead of a post office box number. He thought that looked more professional.

Getting off the bus to check the mailbox meant getting off two stops later, then walking back home. It wasn't that bad, but I asked Mom and Dad if I could have one of those wheeled bags, instead of my backpack. I figured it might get pretty heavy walking back, especially on rough homework nights. They agreed, but said to be sure that I got a receipt. It was a deductible business expense, they explained, since I had to have it because of our new business.

A couple of folks from the event sent us very nice emails, saying to contact them "when we were ready," and that they'd "love to answer any of our questions." And then that was it. They made it into the circular file too.

A few called. Mom said the deal was not to call them right back. Her philosophy was that whatever they did, they would teach their teams to do—so we wanted to see what happened.

A few days past the event we started to get mail in our box. It was interesting to see what came just to Mom, just to Dad, to the family, and even to me. Some had DVDs about the company or other info. One had my dad cracking up—it said "Dear First Name"! He so wanted to call up the guy just to tell him, but Mom said that wasn't our problem. OK, totally at this guy's expense, but we laughed for days.

Sure enough, we heard from Sophie. First, she sent an email addressed to our whole family. She started out by saying she was still sorry she'd crashed into me, and hoped that my broken bones and bruises were healing nicely. Then she said she'd be following up in a week or so. I noticed she'd forgotten to attach the photo of us with Mr. Adler, but Mom said just to send her the thank you response she'd scripted out, but not to remind her. I told you about the Mom/lawyer/Virgo thing, right? Mom's got a plan even for planning to plan. She said she wanted to be fair to everyone, but she wanted to see what sort of follow-up system each person had. I wanted to see the picture...but oh well.

I was riding the bus past our house about a week later when I realized I hadn't contacted my text angel, or heard anything from her. Like I'd told Stephanie, I didn't want to bother her. But I also didn't want her to bail out of neglect, either. I wasn't sure exactly what to say, so as the bus stopped to drop off passengers, I texted:

HBU

This was Stephanie-and-Alex slang, which my text angel seemed to be fluent in, for how are you doing— "How's By You?" After a few minutes, my phone pinged:

lml here 4u -worries hbu

She was "living her life," and "there for me, no worries." That sounded good—sounded like she wasn't pouty that I hadn't texted.

BZ LML2 TTFN <3 <3 <3

She texted me back immediately, not to be outdone:

@>--,-}—'-,--}---

A long-stemmed text rose, obviously answering to the three hearts (<3 <3 <3) I'd sent. She was quick!

I was actually surprised at how busy—"BZ"—I was. Now, I was going to the mailbox, thinking about who was going to be our sponsor after running Mom's gauntlet, keeping up with homework, and having planning meetings with Mom and Dad. There was no time for TV, and not a lot of time for social media either. My friends were a little taken aback when I couldn't comment on the latest reality show or drama, because I'd managed to miss it due to the planning meetings or having my nose buried in some book from Dad's study or podcast about the MLM business. I'd also listen to downloads of the CDs Dad got from the local library on the way to and from school, instead of texting or grumbling about what would happen that day. I guess Automobile University now had an extension—Bus High.

I walked up to the front of the bus as the stop approached, and smiled at Doug, the driver, as he pushed the button to open the door. I wonder if someone like him would try this business? I was still musing about that when I walked into the mailbox store, the bell hanging over the door ringing merrily.

I opened up our mailbox with the key, and inside there was a note to see the woman behind the counter, Juana. She was really nice, but I was puzzled.

I took the paper up to her counter and waited until she finished notarizing something for the man in front of me. As I waited, I scanned to see what was new in the tiny establishment. Juana's always trying to add one more thing for us to buy—she now had shoes on Lucite stands, purses and a new sign that said something in Spanish about phone cards. If she finds an item and can fit it in there and sell it, she will. She'd even taken out the tall table that used to be in the middle for people to read their mail at, and extended out the showcases for jewelry. A smile crossed my face wondering when she'd find a way to string up festive piñatas ("venta especial!") from the high ceiling.

I stepped up to the counter, and Juana smiled before heading to the back.

"Box for you, Miss Alexzandra," she said, handing me a box and a list to sign that I had received it.

"Thanks Juana!" I said cheerily, curious about the box. It was packaged very securely; I'd need a knife to open it. I was pretty sure Juana would have one, but I thought I'd better wait and get it home. I stuffed it in the top of my bag and put the rest of the mail in the outside pocket.

"You're going to need a bigger bag," Juana said back with a lilt, gesturing to a large bright red pull-bag on the end of the row of purses.

I laughed. "Soon!" I said over my shoulder, pulling the door open and jangling the bell. "I have my eye on that one!" She smiled at me as I pulled the door closed and headed for home.

As soon as I got home, I hauled the box, mail, and my homework out of the bag and onto the dining room table. I was "authorized," as Mom put it, to open anything that came to the mailbox. I was always careful how I opened the envelopes, since Mom kept them all in some system in the study.

The mail included some flyers "welcoming" us to our business; Mom had registered Dream Choosers with the county so we could do business legally under that name. I opened the small white cardboard box last. It was actually addressed to me, and wonder of wonders, my name was even spelled right. Inside was a box of brownies, a set of DVDs, and a card. I curiously opened the card and just about fell over. On the front was a photo of Jordan Adler with our family—with a voice bubble coming out of his mouth saying, "the Dream Choosers Team is going to rock the house!" Inside, it said:

Dear Alex,

I hope that you're a chocolate lover like me! It was so great 'running into' you at the event at the Hilton. Yeah I know, ha ha, very funny.

> *So anyway—you might want to take a peek at the DVDs—they talk a bit more about the company. Maybe you'll find them a little dry, maybe not—but brownies have gotta help.*
>
> *I'll give you guys a call next week to see if I can answer any questions—or if you want, you can always give me a ring. I'd be really happy to hear from you.*
>
> *Please give Olivia and Steve my best. You guys are Choosing the Dream—I love that…and I also love how (from your business card) your team name reflects it, too! You go!*
>
> *Best, Sophie*

She'd added her phone number and email address—though we had them from the email and calls she'd made to us already. I started to feel bad that we hadn't returned any of her calls, and that our email response had been just Mom's totally noncommittal scripted one.

I really wanted to give her a call—maybe even tell her what we were doing, sorting for the right person to help us. I also knew that would be a bad idea, considering how serious Mom and Dad were taking all of this and being "fair." So I did what we'd all agreed to—I put what she'd sent us down on our list. DVD, personal card, and brownies.

Everyone was on this list. From the 'you call me' business-card-handing folks, on up. We'd actually gotten a few DVDs and other cards. But brownies were a trump card—and that photo! Wait until Mom and Dad saw this.

Mom had said it was pretty unconventional to do what we were doing. Usually you just signed up with the person who presented you with the opportunity. But she had wound up with a less-than-helpful sponsor when she had done this in her previous MLM. We needed to build this business fast if we were to keep Dad here, and maybe even get me to college in Hawaii. Mom likened it to purchasing a regular business. You wouldn't just sign on the dotted line the first one that you found, even if you liked the person selling it. You'd look at what you were buying, and choose what looked like it would help get you to having profits fastest.

I wondered how many people signed up to do this, but had a sponsor who ignored them, or had their life get in the way—or whatever. My guess was they wound up being the people griping on the Internet about the whole network marketing profession. Mom said that was the "buy and hope" strategy. We had to use something different—because you might say that our life, as we knew it, depended on it.

In the end, the brownies and photo card—combined with her previous easy-going emails and calls—sealed the deal for Sophie. We had narrowed it down to four potential sponsors, but Sophie matched almost everything on our list. She was always helpful—without being desperate—and willing to find the answers to our questions, even when she didn't know them right off. Everyone got the same questions to answer about the company, because Mom wanted to be fair. But Sophie made sure to email us the answer to the questions she didn't know right off the bat within a day. She went the extra mile to include us in her weekly team calls, and invited us to Jordan Adler's team calls. She also sent us some links to a bunch of videos and calls from big money earners in the company, and others on MLM in general.

When she called or emailed, she always ended the same way—"Let me know when you're ready or if you need more time."

Ultimately, though she was out of state, we decided that she was going to be the best sponsor for us.

Once we signed up, Sophie helped us get our company website set up and walked us through understanding the products, how to sign people up, get DVDs—all the things we needed to launch our business. She also made sure we *really* understood what we would do next. She went through the training guide from the company with us, and made it clear that it was all there to share with our team once we got a team going. The idea was to be *duplicatable*—she stressed that repeatedly. If we did things that she and her sponsor and her sponsor's sponsor on up had found to be successful, then everyone should be able to replicate that success through the ranks. Mom stressed that it was also important that the people we signed up did this as well. One was a job, like Mom had done having all those parties in her other MLM, but no one signing up. The other was, as Kiyosaki would say, a B-Business, which would lead to cash flow.

The most interesting part was the phone call and email templates that Sophie shared with us. Mom particularly was impressed with how systematic it was—email a certain note that you could spice up with personalization, call seven days later, questions to ask, things to say, information to be sure you knew about your prospects. I felt a little weird—all that personal stuff Sophie had asked us had really just been to get us to sign on the dotted line?—but Mom explained that no, this is exactly what we wanted. It didn't mean Sophie wasn't interested in us personally; Mom said that's why she'd been so specific about whether the person looked us in the eyes, or how they made us "feel." As Mr. Adler had said, the key to success was to use the company's product, show others how to use it, and keep following up—that's it. The K.I.S.S. —Keep It Simple, Silly— principle in action. Mom explained that this is why Sophie had been so good about the "following up" part—she had a system to make sure she kept in contact. And, Mom also reminded me that this, bottom line, was a business. You should be friendly with people that you are doing business with, but this isn't a social club.

Having a system made it all a lot easier. We just had to follow it. And, most importantly, as I'd heard on one of the company's conference calls, you could work the system either full-time or part-time, but not *some time*. The key was having a system, and following it consistently over time you blocked out each week. Period.

After finally deciding on our sponsor, we were excited to get started. After Sophie showed us the company's system and methods, I couldn't wait to see what would happen next.

Chapter Fourteen

My phone went off at 4 a.m. Ever since my text angel came on the scene, I've charged it right next to my bed, just in case. I didn't want to miss anything. Groggily, I swiped open the phone, holding it close to my face and peering at the screen. I groped for my glasses on the nightstand with the other hand.

It was from Stephanie.

I must not be reading this right, I thought. But I was instantly awake. My free hand landed on my glasses; I picked them up, sat up, and looked at the screen again.

> big d
> mom + me on th way 2 ur house now
> dunno where2 go

Holy cow. Divorce?!

I flipped off the comforter and slipped my feet out from under the sheet to the floor, feeling around with them for my slippers. I wasn't sure what to do. If Stephanie was actually driving over here, there was no reason to text back, as she took the No Phone Zone thing seriously. Just in case, I said:

> K makin java 4u

I pulled on a hoodie and some sweats. Then it dawned on me she'd said she was on her way... with her mom. I'd better get some help. I opened my bedroom door, crossed the hall, and cracked

Mom and Dad's door. I could hear Dad's heavy breathing, but I was counting on "Momdar" to roust Mom without Dad knowing.

"Mom," I breathed, and I heard a rustle. "Mom…" I whispered again a tiny bit louder. I heard her feel around for her glasses, and then the creak of the bed as she slid out.

She came to the door. What a sight we were. Two girls with messed up hair, glasses, retainers—Mom still wore hers at night—great stuff. She shut the door for a second to reach behind it for her robe, then slid out, closing it behind her back.

"I got a text from Stephanie about five minutes ago," I whispered. "It basically said she and her mom are on their way here—that they're getting a divorce and they didn't know where else to go."

Mom's eyes grew somber.

"Well, I guess we'd better make some coffee," she said quietly, then thought for a second. "Do you know if Stephanie's mother drinks?"

It was odd that, though Stephanie and I had been friends for years, our moms didn't hang out. Come to think of it, I wasn't sure I knew Stephanie's Mom's first name.

"She'll have wine with dinner," I said, trying to think.

We headed down the hallway, carefully shutting the hallway door behind us to try to keep Dad from waking up. "This is a Scotch kind of thing. I guess I'll just put something out on the sideboard and see. When did she call?"

I knew what she was thinking. "They should be here pretty soon," I said.

"We'd better get busy."

I put the water on for coffee and filled the Thermos with hot water from the tap to warm it up. Mom reached up above the fridge and got down some bottles of various kinds. She pulled out a silver tray that she'd gotten from her grandma, put the bottles on it, and went into the dining room, putting them on the sideboard. Then she came back, opened up the cabinet, and craned her neck to peer up to the top shelves.

She reached to the very back of the top shelf and pulled down some crystal tumblers. She looked at them critically for dust, grabbed a towel, wiped them, and went into the other room to arrange them next to the silver tray. Next, she opened the freezer and shook the ice tray; I was just pouring the water from the kettle into the coffee filter when we heard Stephanie's car drive up.

"I don't want them to wake your Dad up," Mom said. Then she caught a glimpse of her reflection in the darkened window—retainer, hair, glasses, and of course robe and bare feet. "I've got to put something else on fast," she said quietly, turning down the hall. "Go outside and meet them, so they don't ring the bell," she whispered over her shoulder as she closed the hall door. The smell of the coffee wafted from the stove as I headed out the front door, pushing the lock button so that it wouldn't close and lock me out. That'd be classic.

Stephanie and her mom were getting out of Stef's Mercedes. It was just weird. Stephanie was dressed similar to me, wearing a hoodie and sweats. When her mom opened the passenger door though, I could see she was in an evening dress and heels, with a long black coat over her shoulders. What...?

Stephanie came around the car from the driver's side, put her arm around her mom, slammed the door, then fired the lock button on her keys backwards over her shoulder in one fluid motion. As she came up the path, I could see the fire blazing in her eyes. Whoa.

The streetlight shone on Mrs. Thompson's hair, and not in a flattering way. She had blonde hair that my mom would probably call "out of a bottle," though knowing Mrs. Thompson, if it came out of a bottle, it was an expensive bottle. Her hair always looked brittle, and in that light, under Stephanie's arm, she looked really frail. It was scary.

"We need to keep our voices down," I said in a whisper. "Dad is still sleeping, but Mom's up. OK?" Stephanie nodded—her mom didn't say anything as they came in and I sat them together on one of the living room couches. "I made coffee, do you guys want some?" Stephanie nodded for both of them.

"Cream for me, black three sugars for Mom," she said. I turned and headed to get the coffee.

As I got mugs down from the cabinet, I could hear Mom open the hall door and go into the living room. I filled the mugs, carried two in for Stephanie and Mrs. Thompson first, then went back for two more. Mom had slipped on jeans, thick wool socks and a sweatshirt; her hair was pulled back and her contacts were in.

"Stephanie, I heard that you texted Alexzandra—do you guys want to start from the top?"

My mind was working a mile a minute trying to figure what was going to come next. I sat across from them on the matching couch. Mom sat cross-legged on the floor in front of our fireplace. She was very still. My leg was bouncing up and down like it wasn't under my control. The Big D…? The Thompsons…?

Stephanie looked at her mom, who took a deep breath. But then in typical fashion, Stephanie just went ahead.

"So, Mom and Dad were at a big benefit last night," she started. Her mom sank back into the couch, cradling her mug of coffee. Stephanie stood up and started pacing. She was bursting with energy and it made the room feel electric. My leg bounced like crazy but I held still, watching her go back and forth.

Stephanie continued, "Mom had gone off to the ladies room, and was coming back from behind Dad. One of the catering staff, some young girl, came up to Dad with a tray of champagne, and then did a double-take, saying to him, 'Hey, I recognize you! I work at Auberge part-time—you're the one who comes in with your wife a couple times a month! How is she—how's your wife?' Just then, Mom came up from behind, and said to her, *'I'm* fine—though I've never *been* to Auberge.' The waitress turned deathly white and nearly ran the other direction. Mom asked Dad what was up—and he didn't even deny it." Stephanie's voice rose as she paced and gestured, the coffee in her right hand sloshing dangerously close to the rim. Mom stole an involuntary glance at the hall door, but didn't say anything. It's kind of hard to "shush" someone in a case like this.

"Dad told Mom that she might as well know that he'd been having an affair with someone at work. And she 'really got him', made him 'feel young again.' Mom had no idea—*I* had no idea." I could hear from Stephanie's voice that the second fact was the one that miffed her the most. She was definitely Daddy's Girl. "So they drove home, and by that time Mom was steamed. She was screaming at him to get out of the house when they came in—that's what woke me up." She stopped long enough to take a long sip from her mug. When she started again, it was as if she remembered Dad was still asleep, because her voice was modulated. "Dad said that the house came from his folks and his money and his business—and that he'd do no such thing. By this time, I was downstairs and in the thick of it. So I just grabbed Mom, turned her around, grabbed my phone, and texted you."

My mom let out a long breath. "Can I get you anything stronger?" she asked Mrs. Thompson, gesturing to the sideboard in the dining room. She shook her head, though I think if Mom had asked Stephanie, she would have knocked back a Scotch without even breaking stride in her pacing.

"I didn't even grab my purse," Mrs. Thompson finally said, and her voice was close to tears. "I know that in a few hours, John's going to go to work like nothing happened—maybe even tell this woman that now they can be together." She paused, drawing in a shaky breath. "He said he's going to get our lawyers to draw up papers immediately," she continued. "I can't believe I didn't even know this was going on, right under my nose."

Mom interrupted. "I know a good divorce lawyer," she said, holding up her hand as Mrs. Thompson started to protest. "Listen, if he really is going to get things started, your best defense is a good offense. You need to pull yourself together—you need to see where you stand."

Mrs. Thompson didn't look like she could stand at all. "We have a pre-nup," she said. "I'm not sure how this goes, but I know Stephanie and her sister will be taken care of—I'm just not sure about me." Mom leaned forward and patted the side of Mrs. Thompson's leg in sympathy. What an odd scene: Stephanie pacing and steaming; Mrs. Thompson in her evening gown and heels, slumped on the couch cradling a mug of coffee; Mom cross-legged in jeans on the floor patting Mrs. Thompson's leg; me watching it like a tennis match, frozen except for my bounce-bounce-bouncing leg.

"We got married when I wasn't all that much older than Stephanie's sister, Amelia, is now," Mrs. Thompson continued. "John was everything anyone could want—great family, going somewhere, stable, handsome—the works. When his dad made me sign that paperwork I didn't think anything of it, and John pooh-poohed the whole thing. We were crazy in love. It would never end." Her voice shuddered and she sipped her coffee, then went on. "We met when I was a flight attendant. I'm too old to go back to that—and I don't know anything else. This is just awful." Now she did break down in tears, and Stephanie practically threw herself on her mom in a hug. She'd actually never had that great a relationship with her mom and I always thought kind of looked down on her—but tonight, she was all Mom's Girl.

"Why don't I make us something to eat?" Mom said, nodding to Mrs. Thompson. "When it's a bit later, I'll go with you back to your house, once the girls get off to school." Stephanie gave my mom a *Hell No* look, but it was countered by my mom's *Hell Yes* look, which wilted Steffie. "I don't have much going on at work so we can get some stuff together for you guys, and set you up at the inn for now." Mom's voice was firm, and so both Stephanie and Mrs. Thompson nodded. "Right now, what you have to worry about is talking to a divorce lawyer, and get the process started your way, too. We'll try to find a copy of the pre-nup when we're at your house—and Stephanie, we'll get some stuff for you, but maybe you and Alex can stop by again after school and get anything that I miss." Stephanie and I both nodded, and Mom got up, heading into the kitchen. I headed back into the kitchen to help. Dad would get a big surprise hot breakfast this morning, thanks to all this.

"Can you grab me the eggs, Alexzandra?" Mom said, and then lowered her voice, turning with the frying pan in one hand as she flicked on the stove, "And, what's Stephanie's mom's name…?"

I shrugged, a total blank. Mom took the eggs from me, opened the carton and started cracking them into a bowl.

"Well Sherlock, go and stealth it out. I can't spend the day with her calling her Mrs. Thompson," she said in a mock-stern voice, but smiling slightly. I topped off my coffee and headed back into the living room.

Chapter Fifteen

We got to school super early. Once Dad was awake, he, Mom and Mrs. Thompson—Sarah—started talking about the whole thing. Stephanie was a bundle of fire, and she kept interrupting. I knew I had to get her out of there, so off we went.

Turns out Stephanie hadn't grabbed her purse, book bag, or anything else on her way out of her house—just her keys and her phone. Since we were on the road early I asked Steffie if she wanted to stop by her house to grab anything, but she didn't want to run into her dad. Stephanie's a little crazy, but serious about stuff like driving without a license, so I got to get behind the wheel of the Roadster. Man, I might have to add one to my 'goals' list for our business; I was never much of a car person but this was sweet! We agreed on a rendezvous for lunch—Mom had actually packed us both one since she wasn't rushing to work.

"What's going on with Stephanie?"

I was at my locker toward the end of third period when Charlie came up from behind me. This was only about the twentieth time I had answered the question already today. "Big D," I said to Charlie. He gasped.

"No." Charlie breathed out.

"Yeeees," I said, banging my locker closed and twirling the dial. We walked down the hall toward the stairs; we had Chemistry together. "She and her mom came over this morning before like, dawn. Mom's handling the situation."

Charlie had to smile at that—Mrs. Thompson couldn't have a better person on her side than my mom during a time like this.

"She's going to set them up at the hotel for now and get someone she knows to help them out," I continued. We walked along for a bit without talking, surrounded by the roar of students and teachers getting to their next classes, slamming lockers, sneakers squeaking on the floor, friends calling out over the din to others, laughter, grumbling.

"Mom says you guys are getting started on that business thing," Charlie said after a bit. "She's still not crazy about it, but she said that after your mom talked to her, it does sound better than the last time."

I had to think for a second—I had totally forgotten about our new business. Maybe this was how people got sidetracked. Life comes at you and gets in the way, so you forget about what you're aiming for.

"Man, that whole thing got so knocked out of my head! In fact, catch you inside," I said to Charlie, as I spied Lenardo Gonzales heading toward his Physics class. I jogged to catch him.

I'd approached Lenardo when we were going to see Jordan Adler at the meeting in the city, and unlike the folks who teased me about wanting to get into a "pyramid scheme," Lenardo had actually been curious to hear about what I'd learned. Lenardo is cute, dresses really nice—overall, he seemed to work really hard. His dad stood on the side of the road to get labor work for ten dollars an hour and lunch—In fact, neither of his parents spoke much English. He didn't run with a gang like his younger brother, or sell drugs like his older one. He was polite, always sitting at the front in class and studying hard. My guess was that high school was it for him, because how could he afford college? But it was obvious he was trying to break out and move up.

"Hey!" I said, surprising him. He turned around and looked a bit blankly at me—as if he had been in the middle of doing a physics problem in his head. But his face brightened when he saw me.

"Alexzandra! ¿Qué pasa?!" he said, and I grinned.

"Lo mismo," I answered. "Hey, actually, listen, I want to talk to you for a couple seconds," I said. He looked puzzled, so I added, "Nothing bad, honest, I want to get your thoughts on something—no worries." He looked at me expectantly, so I just launched on in. "My folks and I are getting started in this new thing, and I wanted to get your take on it."

"What kind of thing?" he asked, his brow wrinkling.

"It's that business," I said. "The short story is that my dad is trying to keep from being transferred, and you can do it from your home or anywhere. I told my folks I would mention it to people I thought might be interested here, and they are going to talk to their friends too."

Lenardo smiled. "This is that thing you were talking about before, right?" he asked. "The thing you went to the city to hear about?"

"Yeah that's it."

"So it looks as good as you thought?" he asked.

"You know, seriously? I'm not sure," I said. "I think so, but I wonder how broad interest in something like this could be? We did sign up for it, and so we have a website and some information and stuff like that. I was curious whether you'd check it out and let me know what you think?" I really wanted his opinion so I could see whether this just looked good from our standpoint, or if it would appeal to other people different than our family.

"Yeah, totally," he said. I reached into my back pocket and pulled out one of the business cards and wrote our personal website on the back. Lenardo gave me that turned down mouth, big eyes, upshot eyebrows *look at you* glance when I handed him the printed card.

"All this information is good, it just doesn't have the website on it. Which by the way, the company gives you for free when you sign up to do the business."

"Oh, that reminds me," Lenardo said unzipping his bookbag. "I have that book you loaned me," he continued, pulling out *Rich Dad, Poor Dad*. "The coolest part is, I went online and there were copies in Spanish, so I got one for Mom and Dad, and also a copy of *The Cashflow Quadrant*. They're reading them now. I can hear them when Dad gets home from working, discussing the concepts. They actually sound super excited—and have been trying to talk about what a 'B-Business' as Kiyosaki puts it really is. Mom always tries to do what she can, and Dad works like crazy—but they realize that they're just working a job, day to day, and if they stop the money stops. They really didn't think there was a way that people like them could do anything different. Do you think that the thing you want me to look at could be a "B" for people like my parents?"

I thought for a second. "It's pretty easy to explain, and I bet you that there is stuff in Spanish—I just never thought to look." I was mad at myself—I should have thought of that.

"No te preocupes," he said, seeing my expression. "It's not exactly something that you would think of like I would. And that's why you want me to look at this—different perspective, right? I'll check it out tonight and see what I think," he said, as the warning bell rang before class. I walked nonchalantly down the hallway until he was inside his class, then rushed down the hall and around the corner toward Chemistry, knocking straight into Josh.

"Hey!" he said, surprised. "So what's up with Stephanie?" I shook my head and raced past.

"Late, gotta go, we'll be in the caf at lunch," I shouted over my shoulder as my dash became a sprint to my class. But I had another thought. Wonder if Josh would be interested in an opportunity that wouldn't involve changing tires?

Chapter Sixteen

A light knocking on my bedroom door woke me from my late morning snooze. I reached for my glasses and glanced at the clock—nine in the morning. I stretched as Mom came into the room—with a smile and a cup of coffee. I'd come home from school and pretty much fell into bed; I'd been up since our 4 a.m. drama.

"OK you," Mom said, and I smiled at the tone in her voice. My guess was that she was going to somehow commend me on how I had handled the Stephanie/Mrs. Thompson thing. Not sure why that rated coffee in bed, but I wasn't about to complain. "Who's Eduardo Gonzales?"

"What?" Still groggy, I couldn't figure out what the heck she was talking about. Mom cracked up at my crinkled-up face under what I was sure was a spectacular bed head after double-digits of sleep. This is how Dad loved to see her, his eyes always went soft—Mom with her hair in a ponytail and her freckles, eyes above sparkling and dancing.

"Sophie called us this morning," she said. I remembered the phone ringing—in fact, that's what really woke me up, then I'd just snuggled down into weekend snooze mode. "We have our first team member! Eduardo Gonzales. We knew you had to have signed him up, since your dad was at work all day and I was with Sarah Thompson. What the heck were you up to, Miss Businesswoman?"

The light bulb went off. Lenardo! I sat straight up in bed, a jet of excitement juicing through me. "No way! You're kidding—that's amazing!" I said, as Mom handed me the coffee and sat on the foot of my bed. I took a sip, shaking my head. Then I launched into the story—Lenardo's background, about his brothers, his dad and mom, the Kiyosaki books, the whole deal. Mom paid rapt attention.

"So this isn't really someone you know all that well either—like Stephanie or Charlie?" she asked.

I shook my head.

"This is exactly what we are doing this for," she said, nodding. "It sounds like you really thought about the opportunity, and who it could benefit. I am so proud of you!" My dad would have ruffled my hair at that moment; Mom just beamed. "Sophie said that we should give them a call to welcome them to the team. What do you think about that?"

I pondered for a second. "Well, I'm pretty sure that Lenardo's parents don't speak English all that well. Maybe you should have Dad call." My dad had done a study abroad program in Mexico City and his Spanish was pretty good. "I'm not sure I would want to make the call . . . you don't want *me* to do it, right?" I asked, suddenly feeling a little shy.

"That's OK," Mom said, and for a second I thought she really might ruffle my hair. "I think that your Dad and I should probably talk to his parents anyway, maybe meet them in person. Sophie says that really making your team feel like they did the right thing from the outset is important." She shook her head and smiled, looking down and picking a little at my comforter. "I am just so proud of you, Alexzandra!" she said. "I worked at that other MLM for a year, and never signed up one person. This is just so awesome!"

"Of course, the funniest part is how Sophie called."

I looked at her quizzically, and she took in a quick breath through her nose, suppressing a laugh at herself.

"Sophie must check on her computer every morning—she saw immediately that we had a new distributor, and called to give us kudos," Mom said. "I of course started arguing immediately that No, we didn't have any distributors." I started chuckling at that—I could just see it. "I told her that I didn't even remember how to get *in* to see that. So, she patiently showed me again. I am glad that she made a point of setting up our website—and that you remembered the address for it! Your dad is going to be razzing me all day for trying to talk Sophie out of the fact that we had a distributor."

"Well, what do you think I should do if you're calling Mr. and Mrs. Gonzales?" I asked as she got up and headed for my bedroom door. She stopped, thinking.

"Well, I'll show you the back office on the website; all their information is there. Remember how much you liked that Sophie sent you that card and brownies? Maybe you should do that for Lenardo."

I thought about it and smiled, throwing back the comforter. So much for more lazing around—I had work to do! Mom had already headed out my bedroom door—but then she stepped back in.

"Oh, I meant to say," she smiled. "Your dad and I feel that you should get the check for the Gonzales family signing up. You can do what you want with it—but it's your work, so you should get the benefits." My mouth actually dropped open. Combined with the bed head, glasses, retainer, I'm sure it was a sweet look.

Mom laughed. "Yeah, seriously," she said, turning out the door. "You're going to be there for Lenardo, we will be there for his folks. But hey, way to go, girl!"

My mind was racing; I need to make a list or something. I'd thought of Josh yesterday—who else?

Chapter Seventeen

Monday was here before I knew it. I saw Lenardo in the hall, and he was superexcited at how his folks had jumped on the business. He said his mom was already talking to her sister, cousin, and best friend about it. His dad was going to see how to approach some of the guys who did what he did—day labor. Lenardo walked with a real bounce in his step, and couldn't stop talking about how his folks were reacting. Just being with him made me excited, too.

I had agreed to have lunch with Stephanie. She and her mom were back in their house as of today—something to do with Mom's friend who was now their attorney.

"It was really nice of your mom to make lunches for us the other day," she said as she sat down with her standard gigantic mocha, some chips, and a candy bar. I always wondered if her mom just gave her money for lunch and, if she did, if she'd be a little shocked at where it went.

"You know, my mom is freaking," she said. "She hasn't had to work for, like, decades. Dad always took care of her. Now, I'm sure that we're going to be fine—but they're totally Splitsville," she continued. "I mean this is only like a couple days, but Mom and her lawyer were together nearly all weekend. I think we're selling the house once I'm at college. Dad will still pay for college and grad school—or whatever, but he's all weird. It's a nightmare." Stephanie shook her head, crinkling the top of the candy wrapper with her blinged-out fingernails. "He keeps texting me. He wants to have coffee with me tonight. He wants to talk. I don't know how to. I always kinda thought that Mom was no big deal, Dad and I were tight. Now he does this, I have to be there for Mom, I don't want to do that, I want to be…well, I just want to be oblivious." She took a sip of her mocha and paused, thinking.

"I really don't think there's a chance they will get back together," she continued. "Mom pretty much went from flight attendant to society and now, well, who is she? Think about it—she's at the Club because Dad's a member. It's not like she could afford what they do on her own. I don't even want to think about this. I don't want to have to think about her, I want to think about me." She pouted—I almost laughed. From anyone else this would sound selfish and vain—but the fact Stephanie was saying anything even a bit self-reflective was a wonder. "Hey," she continued, obviously trying to change the subject, "What's up with your text angel? Think she would have some advice from the ether-sphere for me?"

I hadn't even thought about my text angel for a while. Things were so busy, especially now with the added extra of the business stuff. I shrugged. "I'm not sure Steffie," I said, taking a chip out of her bag and crunching it. "Do you want me to ask? I mean—ask what?"

She thought. "I don't know," she said, spinning the chip bag back around and taking a chip out for herself. "I guess not. I just wish I knew what was going to happen next."

"I think that you're going to be OK," I said, because I did. "Look, honestly you're going to be fine. Your dad might try to convince you that what he's doing is right, but I don't think that you have to worry. You're still his little girl, and always will be. He's going to pay for college. So you're going to be fine."

She mused. "What if they get married? What if they have kids?"

I hadn't actually thought about that part. "Look," I said, and leaned back in the plastic chair. "If that happens it's going to be way in the future. You're going to be at least in college. Things change. You can figure that out when it happens, if it happens."

I looked up at Stephanie, and saw her friend Jaycee making a beeline for her from behind. I don't know Jaycee that well—she's someone Stephanie knows from her folks' Club.

"Stepha-NEEE!" Jaycee said as she approached Steffie, her French-manicured nails wrapped around a coffee cup. Stephanie perked up, turned around, and I could see the façade slam back up. Her insecurities were safe with me, I thought, but not with people like Jaycee.

Steffie squealed "Jay-CEEEEE!" and stood up to air-kiss her friend and do a little happy dance. Smiling at Jaycee I picked up my notebook; she came around the table and gave me one of those big, fake hugs, leaning down over me and my chair. "Al-lex!" she breathed, plopping her Ernest Sewn jeans'd bootie down in the extra chair at our table.

"I gotta jet, sweeties," I said in a bright voice, giving a bit of a sarcastic beauty queen's wave as I got up. Stephanie didn't even notice the tone. Her laser eye lock was on Jaycee, and I knew why. Jaycee's mom had been dumped by her dad a couple years back. Back then, Stephanie'd had little sympathy for Jaycee, behind her back. Now, she'd want to get all the info. Funny how things change.

That got me thinking about Stephanie's mom—even Jaycee's mom. If there was some sort of support group for people like them, I wonder if Mom could talk to them about the business, to get them back on their feet. Mrs. Thompson's lawyer had said that in a support group, Stephanie's mom would find folks just like her. I'd think they'd need to investigate a new plan for the new direction of their newly single lives. I took out my phone to text Mom the idea as I headed out of the cafeteria.

With my head down, I passed right by Josh, though I could see someone standing near me. I looked up, and then did a double take.

"Well at least this time you didn't try to knock me down," he said.

I laughed. "Hey, I was late," I said, finishing the text and putting my phone in my back pocket. Then I thought—what the heck, no time like the present.

"Where you headed?" I said, and he gestured his thumb back toward the lockers. I fell into step with him. "Aren't you 18?" I started, which made him snort.

"What, you want me to buy you a pack of smokes?" he said incredulously, and I just laughed.

"Oh heck no," I said, "but I want to talk to you about something. I want you to have an open mind about this, and I'm really curious about what you think." He looked sideways, and raised an eyebrow.

"Shoot." I explained the business to him in about a minute—since he was 18, he could sign up himself if he wanted. "Sounds too good to be true, Alex-zander-ah," he said, but I could see he was thinking.

"I know. I get it. But will you check it out?" I had put our website on the back of all my business cards during the weekend—so now I could just pull one out. He started to tease about the card, but I think something in my face made him stop. "Look," I said seriously. "I think I know about you. I mean, I don't know-know, but I think I do. You're a good student," I said, holding up my hands as he rolled his eyes as if I was crazy. "And you say you're going to Mike's Tires. What if something like this could work for you instead? What if you don't have to go be just an employee? What if there's something else?" I handed him the card. "Look, just go to the website that's on the back. It talks about the whole thing, walks you through. I'll call you tonight if you want, to talk it over. Text me when you've looked at it if you want to talk."

"I have bowling tonight," he said, but in an absent-minded voice.

"It's not going to take long to see what this is about," I said. "And my mom and dad are doing this—this isn't some shady cyber scam. I've told you about my mom—she is Ms. Research. She looked into it; it's on the up-and-up. So, when you get home from bowling, you should take a look. I'm talking about the rest of your life."

On Thursday night, Dad and Mom met with Mr. and Mrs. Gonzales in town after Mr. Gonzales was done with work. In just a week they had signed up two more people. Mom and Dad wanted to be sure they didn't have any questions, figuring it would be easier in person. When they got home, I was still up—I couldn't have slept, not until I found out how it went. Mom and Dad were jazzed. They said that Lenardo's parents were so excited about this combined with the '*Padre Rico*' stuff; they were starting a group in their neighborhood based on *Rich Dad* and its principles. Basically, as Dad explained it, they wanted to start a group that showed folks that you could get out—that there was more to life than living day-to-day.

Friday after Economics class with Mr. Sherman, I hung back. I had spoken to him after class a couple times when I was reading the *Rich Dad* books. He was approachable and able to tie it into what we were discussing in class. I'd even talked to him about Dad's job circumstances, which had led to discussing employment in general as it related to the current economic situation. But this would be my first experience talking to an adult about the actual business opportunity. After everyone had banged out of class and into the weekend, I approached his desk.

"Mr. Sherman?" I asked, and he looked up.

"Yes Alexzandra?" he replied, through his thick brown beard.

"Do you remember a couple weeks back when I was telling you about my dad's job and that business thing my folks were considering?"

He leaned back in his desk chair, looking thoughtful. "I know we talked a little about teachers' salaries and trading cash now for the hope of a pension later," he said, "a bit to my chagrin actually."

I smiled. "No worries," I said, pulling my thumb and middle finger closed against my lips as if to 'zip' in a secret. "Safe with me. I'm curious, because my mom and dad did start that business, and it seems to be really working for some folks who are looking for a Plan B. I wondered if you'd want to take a peek at it."

Mr. Sherman looked skeptical. "I know you're trying to be helpful," he said, "but I think I'm too old to do something like that. I don't have a lot of time, what with grading papers, meetings, stuff like that."

I persisted. "I hear you, but you know, the thing is, that this is a way to maybe get a little extra in your pocket for working part-time. All I'm wondering is whether you'd take a look—and especially from an economics perspective, I'd be really curious about your thoughts."

He still looked skeptical, but I ripped out a page from my notebook and wrote our website address on it. I didn't want it to look too professional or like I was this total businessperson or anything, especially to an adult—so I kept the business cards in my pocket. "Hmmmm," he said, looking at the website name. "How long is this going to take?"

"Honestly, it's like 20 minutes," I said. "If you click on the first part you can see the background on the company, how it got started, and then it talks about the compensation plan. That's the part I'd like to get your help on." I had a flash of intuition. "I don't exactly get how the compensation plan works, and I know you could explain it to me, which I would really appreciate."

Mr. Sherman picked up the note, putting it in the top of his briefcase and snapping the brass locks closed. "OK, I'll take a look," he said. "Frankly, I'm a little curious to see how one of these companies works. Why not? Do you want to talk about it on Monday? I will look this weekend."

Awesome! I was sure he wasn't putting me on. Heck, maybe he could be my first adult distributor!

Riding home, I leaned my head against the bus window and scrolled through my Playlist, queuing up the latest personal development audio I'd downloaded. Just then my phone rang—it was Sophie! I hate it when people in public places blab like no one else is around, but I was halfway back on the bus and it was empty. I still kept my voice down.

"I was just thinking of you!" I said, and I'm sure she could hear the happiness in my voice.

"What up girl!" she said in her sunny voice that made me smile. "Congrats on your team building. You are a natural!" I laughed. I liked the sound of that, though I mean, come on—how hard is it to point someone in the direction of a website and ask them what they thought? "So, listen," she continued, "I'm not sure if you guys have seen this, but there's a trip coming up. All the details are on the website—it might be a fun goal to have. The company pays for everything. It could be fun! Of course not just because I'm going…" she let her voice trail off.

"Where's it to?" I said, curious. What a 'job' this was—you worked at something you believed in, got cashflow income, and there were trips, too?

"Hawaii," she said, and I sat up in the seat.

"No way. Really?" The people in the car next to the bus could probably hear me. So much for keeping my voice down.

"Really! You should look at the rules, but I bet you guys could totally do it. How great would that be?" she asked, and there was no other answer but…

"Awesome!"

Once we were off the phone, I was totally daydreaming. An all-expenses paid trip to Hawaii? I would have to check that out as soon as I got home. I didn't care what I had to do—I was going to do it!

I got off to check our mailbox as usual, waved to Juana and unlocked our box. Inside, there was just one envelope—it was from the company. Curious, I decided to open it there. I pulled the letter out and unfolded it, then let out a little gasp. It was our first check! Actually it was *my* check! It had the Gonzales' name on the lower part, and was made out to our team, "Dream Choosers." I couldn't believe it!

I thought a bit, and actually took a long look at the cool red pull-bag that Juana had pointed out to me a while back. With this check I could buy it and still have money left over. But as Mom had explained to me, we had to deposit the checks we got, then take the money out and keep track of it all in a business-like way. She'd brought the legal paperwork that showed we could use Dream Choosers as a business name to our bank, so we could deposit checks when "they came rolling in." Well—here was our first one!

I went over to the bank to deposit the check. It felt like I'd just deposited a million dollars, rather than a couple hundred. I almost skipped on the way home. Hey, I said 'almost.'

Chapter Eighteen

I headed to Mr. Sherman's room with my lunch at noon on Monday. He wasn't there yet, so I went over the rules that I'd printed off the website for the Hawaii trip and my plans to get there.

I was super excited once I'd figured out the rules, and saw that we really *could* do it. By the time Mom and Dad got home Friday, I was just about jumping out of my skin to tell them. When I laid it out step by step, Dad nodded and pursed his lips. I could see that he thought we could do it, too. He turned to Mom, saying, "She certainly is your daughter in the planning department!"

Sure, I knew that keeping Dad from having to move to Tennessee was more important than any contest. But it was cool that moving in that direction would be rewarded *by* the contest. It was like you got a benefit for just doing what you should be doing anyway.

"Alexzandra!" said Mr. Sherman as he came into the room, interrupting my reverie. He left the door open, and took a seat at his desk. Then, as if he thought better of it, he got up and sat at the student desk next to the one I was in, bringing his lunch from his briefcase with him. I liked that. It made me feel more like an equal.

"Hey Mr. S," I said as he sat down. "So, did you get a chance to take a look?"

He nodded. "I watched everything," he said. "And I can definitely see how this might be of interest, especially to people I know," he said, taking a bite from an apple.

"Does the whole compensation plan make sense?" I asked. "I keep getting people calling it a pyramid scheme and I don't really know what to say."

"Well, this is definitely not a pyramid scheme," he said. "A pyramid is where people pay in money, and that's the same money that is paid out to people who are getting checks. Like Social Security is now—remember how we talked about that in class?"

I nodded. "Well, sort of," I said. "That there is really no money that is being saved for them for later, that people get what the current people are putting in now. Is that what you mean?"

"Yes, that's it," he said. "In a pyramid, if you don't keep getting more fresh money in, then the checks stop coming to the people getting money paid out. You need more and more people to buy in, to keep paying out. That's what all the scandals were about in the early part of this century. Here, you get a portion of the amount that people spend—like you are the sales person for the company and get a commission. But, unlike being in a corporation, where, to move up, someone else in the company above you has to leave and you have to play politics, here, you can move up as fast as you have time to put in. The way it's set up, you can even pass your sponsor or make more than they do—especially if you sign up someone who gets very involved in the business."

I thought about Mr. and Mrs. Gonzales. Mom said that they were adding people so fast, she was feeling guilty she hadn't signed up anyone yet!

"I'd like to talk to your folks," he said. "I'm just not sure I'm really cut out to be a salesman, which I think you have to be to do this. I'm an economics teacher."

I smiled. "I think that you're a great salesman Mr. Sherman. I mean, think about it. You have to 'sell' economics to us. You're even explaining to me, using economics, why this business is a great opportunity. I think people would listen to you. It's not a guy with a comb-over and a polyester suit, saying 'Is this Mr. Shear-man?' on your phone at dinner time."

"Well, when you put it that way…" he chuckled. "Can I get your folks' number? I would like to give them a ring, and talk it out."

I wrote their info and names on a scrap of paper, put the rest of my lunch in my bag, and headed for the door. Once again, I didn't use our business card, because I thought that as a kid it might look odd. Sophie had taught us that you have to make your prospects feel comfortable, and approach them as they are— and as they believe *you* are. "I really appreciate you helping me understand this," I said. I figured it couldn't hurt to make him feel like a teacher, and like he really 'got' it already. "It makes me feel a lot better about what we're doing."

"That's what we're here for," he said as I left.

"Yeah, I just don't think so." Josh leaned back against the cement wall of the Quad. "There's gotta be a catch."

"Well, the catch is that you do have to work it at least part-time—it's not a ton of dough at the beginning, but eventually it keeps bringing in money even if you're not really working it. Wouldn't it be better to spend some time building up something like this for yourself, than to build up a business for someone else, by being an employee?"

Josh shook his head. "Look, serious? I gotta get out of the house. I've got to get money in now to get my own place. This isn't going to do it for me."

"OK, I can respect that," I said. "But if you work it, even part-time, then ultimately you will be making money that's not just tied to your own labor, but also people you bring into it. Then you could fire your boss, and continue on with it full time, once it's got legs."

He gave me the stone face. "It's not for me, Alex," he said. "I hear you and understand what you're saying. But I can't just take a flyer this will work. I need something that as soon as I'm out of school I can do and break out. Buy a car. Get an apartment. Get a life. I have to be real." Then he put on his loud, prankster, big-man-on-campus voice, changing the subject. "So are you on for Senior Cut Day?" he asked, and I knew that was the end of our talk. I mentally crossed him off my list for Hawaii—but in doing so, I felt like I was crossing him off a list for a life of his own choosing. We kidded around for a bit, but it just made me feel worse. I made an excuse, and headed off to grab a bottle of water before break ended.

I was still thinking about Josh as I boarded the bus to head home. I'd learned a lot on Mr. Adler's and Sophie's team calls. In fact, a couple weeks ago Mr. Adler had talked about how FEAR—which he said stands for False Evidence Appearing Real—ruled so many people's lives. That everything was motivated by either Fear or Love - that you were always either running away from, or towards, something. And the feeling in your gut told you which it was.

I guess that Mom and Dad were driven to succeed because of Fear in a way—their fear of losing Dad's income or him moving to Tennessee. But as we got more into it, though of course that drive was still there, the pleasure of introducing others to something that could really help them out started to shine through.

Josh had to get out from his home life, and he couldn't see anything farther down the road than that. The thing was, as Mr. Kiyosaki and Mr. Trump had said in their book that I'd gotten out of Dad's den, this seemed to be the mindset of 99% of people out there. This didn't feel good to me at all; in fact, it made my stomach hurt. Josh's decision was being based on Fear. I could almost hear the door of his life creaking slowly closed. OK, totally melodramatic, but can't you see it? Josh, ten years from now? Twenty? How about me? See what I mean?

I flashed my pass at the bus driver, Doug, who smiled. The bus wasn't full, but there were a couple handfuls of people scattered throughout. I wanted to call Sophie to talk about Josh, but there really wasn't a quiet way to do it. I took the seat directly behind Doug, figuring I'd try to chat him up about the business. Why not? He actually gave me an opening.

"I've heard you talking about this business thing to other students on the bus," he said. "How can I check it out?"

I was surprised, but I tried not to look like it. "It's pretty easy," I said. "We have a website that can walk you through getting some free product. It also shows you about earning money by doing what we're doing."

Doug nodded. "I have to go out for knee surgery coming up," he said. "I'm going to be out for a while, so I wonder if I could get something like this going while I'm laid up."

"I don't see why not," I said. I handed him my business card over his shoulder. He glanced at it before putting the bus in gear.

"I'm not much of a salesman," he said. I assured him that wasn't really that important, you just used the product, introduced others to try it out, and then followed up to see what they thought.

He was sort of my captive, so I talked about the product, about the company, about the compensation plan, stuff like that. I knew this would be such a great side business for him. He kept looking back at me—but I think he was glad to say, "Here's your stop!" when we drew up by Juana's mailbox place. He smiled at me as I left, but I saw out of the corner of my eye that he folded up my business card and threw it in the trash by his feet.

    I was steamed—I mean, this would be such a good deal for him! But Sophie always said to say as little as possible to get folks interested; the more you said, the more they'd glaze over. I think I just talked him right out of it. Live and learn, I thought. Man, I hate that saying. Live and Freakin' Learn.

Chapter Nineteen

Several months went by and we worked the business when we could. Mom signed up some folks at her firm and the counter person at her dry cleaner. Dad and I looked for opportunities everywhere—at the gym, his job, school. Mr. Sherman did sign up, but Dad said that he was so full of fear about "selling" and "bugging people" that he wasn't sure whether anything would ever come of it.

The Gonzales family kept at it. I realized that with a few more people, they would be on the Hawaii trip before we were! I mentioned it to Lenardo, who was very surprised. His parents hadn't really gone that deeply into the company website—they just explained the product and the opportunity to their friends and had meetings, but didn't know there was more so I gave him the link. After that, every time he passed me in the hallway he made hand motions like a hula dancer and hummed *Aloha 'Oe*.

Stephanie was pretty much back to herself. Her mom did get into a support group, which my mom visited to talk about what having a 'business' meant. She wanted to talk very generally about the idea of having a legitimate home-based business, but not specifically about the one we had chosen. She just wanted them to know this sort of thing was out there. Stephanie's Mom had talked about becoming a travel agent, a personal trainer—lots of things—but each of them sounded to me like being self-employed. Mom figured that she'd talk to the ladies about the whole network marketing profession, answer questions, then let them make their own decisions, presenting our opportunity if they wanted information on it.

Dad spent more time in Tennessee—he even signed a few folks up out there, but you can only build things so fast. Sometimes it felt like we were all burning the candle at both ends, but I remembered what Jordan Adler had said—the most important part, above all, was consistently working the business over time. So we did—short-term working toward Hawaii, but long-term toward financial freedom.

I'd been accepted to a few universities that had agreed to let me start in a later semester—one was the University of Hawaii. I knew going there was a little unlikely—it would take me a couple years to get enough profit to make tuition, not to mention Dad's needing to replace his income. I was feeling a little down. People that turned me down would sometimes call it a "Get Rich Quick Scam." Quick? That was a laugh. But Mom kept saying this was just the way it was supposed to go—slow and steady.

So I kept checking the mailbox, depositing checks, talking to people, getting turned down, getting questions. Some folks signed up all excited at first, but then did nothing. My bus driver, Doug, had gone out to get his surgery; I made friends with André, the substitute driver, and managed to hold my tongue long enough to get him interested in the business. Live and learn.

One evening I was tooling around on our website's back office while I was waiting for the microwave to indicate that my dinner was done—Mom and Dad were out. I heard the "ping" from the kitchen and got up to get it, but then sat back down as I saw a new distributor pop up on our back office. And I just about missed the chair because I sat down so fast.

Mrs. Mellici?

My guidance counselor? You've *got* to be kidding me! And wonder of wonders, Mr. Sherman had signed her up! I went to our email, and sent our template email congratulating Mr. Sherman for signing up his first team member. Then, I sent an email to Mrs. Mellici, welcoming her and letting her know if she had any questions that we were there to help. She wouldn't know it was from me—our emails came from Dream Choosers. I couldn't wait to get to school to talk to Mr. Sherman.

The next morning I stood outside Mr. Sherman's locked room, waiting for him to show. He came around the corner, concentrating on his keys.

"Mr. Sherman!" I said, and he about dropped his keys he was so startled. "Oh sorry," I said. "Look, I'm just totally excited, 'cause I saw that you signed someone up last night!"

He actually smiled, and looked a little pleased with himself.

"We had a staff meeting yesterday after classes, and Beatrice—Mrs. Mellici—was there," he said, getting the key in the lock and turning the knob. "She's not exactly the friendliest of people; I'm not sure why she's a counselor." He flicked on the lights, then turned around as I struggled to hide my 'Yeah, no joke' expression. "I should *not* have said that," he said in a shocked voice, and I laughed, making the 'zipped mouth' hand gesture. "Before Joe—Mr. Melton—got there to call the meeting to order, I was telling a couple of the other teachers about the whole idea of having a Plan B income as a supplement. Beatrice was listening, obviously. At the end of the meeting, she tells me that her mom needs to go into a nursing home, and they're trying to figure out how to pay for it. She wondered if they could make a few extra hundred dollars a month. That will be the difference between a good facility and a substandard one."

Wonder of wonders, who would have known? I thought.

"So, I gave her my website," Mr. Sherman continued. "Thank goodness your parents were so adamant that I get everything set up." He put his briefcase on his desk, turning back toward me.

"I really didn't think I could do it," he said, shaking his head. "But I guess part of this is just being in the right place at the right time, and it takes someone else being in the right place to hear what you say."

"And then you have to just keep saying it." I chimed in. He took his jacket off and put it on the back of his chair.

"That's the best news I've had all month!" His eyes were twinkling. "You're going to be late, you better go." As I turned toward the door, he called me back.

"Hey—seriously—thanks, Alex," he said.

Chapter Twenty

It was slow, but our team kept growing. And it was unbelievable to see how it worked. Mrs. Mellici enlisted her mother, who was at the nursing home. Her mom started talking about it to all the staff, doctors, and visitors. She would stop people in the hall, Mr. Sherman told my mom. And we all watched with astonishment as Mrs. Mellici's "branch" on our genealogy grew—and not just with staff and patients, but with doctors, too. Doctors! That got me thinking.

Charlie had told me that his dad often came home complaining that he could only see patients for three minutes at a time. On top of that, because of all the insurance hoops, he only got slightly more than the patient's co-pay when all was said and done. Though jobs like his and my mom's were the ones people envied from afar for their big salaries, when you thought about it, there was a big cost.

Mr. Sherman signed up our principal, Joe Melton. Then Mr. Melton signed up Miss Young, my English teacher. I hadn't even mentioned it to her; I had thought there was no way she would go for it.

Mom eventually signed up Steffie's mom, then Mrs. Thompson got people in her divorce group to consider it—and even got some folks from the country club. Kind of like the doctors, you'd think that folks with money would be totally down on this stuff. But, as Mom explained it, they were really the ones who understood about jumping on an opportunity. Rich people were all about cash flow opportunities, she said. If only the rich kids at school knew what their parents were finding interesting, they might not turn up their noses quite so much when I tried to explain the business to them!

Dad actually signed up vendors that he worked with through his job. Some of them signed up to just use the product, but some wanted a little bit of extra income, too. Jordan Adler had told us once you get to 100 distributors on your team things really started to happen. We weren't there yet, but after checking the back office one evening, I realized we were on track to make the trip to Hawaii!

Ultimately, my part of the business had to slow down a bit, what with finals, graduation and all that came with it. A lot of us started to realize the few months, then weeks, at the end of senior year were our last as the top of the heap. Though you could hold off going to college, no matter what, everyone had to move on to whatever came next.

I thought about all this, while heading down to the administrative offices for my senior exit interview with Mrs. Mellici. I hadn't seen her since months and months ago, when she'd given me the stink eye about the whole delayed entrance college thing and our business. Funny how things change.

I took a seat in the chairs outside the counselors' offices, and looked at the brass plaque on Mr. Melton's door. It said in fancy script, *Joseph P. Melton, Principal.* Principal—and businessman! I smiled. Though he hadn't built much of a team, he sure used the product. When our monthly check came out detailing the bits and pieces that came from our downline's product purchases, he always was on it. Thanks, Dude, I thought.

I fidgeted in my seat waiting for Mrs. Mellici. Mom and I had discussed what I should do with the college acceptances. Oddly enough, I felt like I had a handle on it, even though I was still just a kid. When I talked to Charlie and Steffie or my other friends about where they were going, they all had some idea that in another four years (or more, if they were going for like law or business or med school), they would "start" something or "be" something.

I knew I was "something" right now. I knew I had a skill where I could get out and make a living. I didn't have to depend on a paycheck, either. Our downline wasn't supporting our family—yet—but I could see that it could.

We were still in what Mr. Adler had said on one of his conference calls was "phase one"—where we were doing a lot more work than we had money coming in. But we could actually see "phase two"—that's where Sophie was—where your energy about equaled your income. In a way, that's where people in a regular job started; their paycheck was exchange for their energy working. So I could at least see how folks like Josh would say that starting with a business like this was worse than if you 'just got a job,' and also why Mr. Adler stressed that it was best to work on this part time while you kept your 'day job.' He even quoted a story by a network marketing legend named Jim Rohn, where Mr. Rohn kept his job until he was making more than three times his salary from his MLM business... because it made such a good story!

And that was the whole deal—"phase three." That's where you are making a lot more money than the effort you're expending. It takes working the business consistently, but that's where people like Mr. Adler were. He still introduced folks to the business, but the check he got monthly was way more than most folks made in a year. And that was his *Beach Money*—like the title of his book. Money he got that wasn't tied to his personal efforts.

I heard Mrs. Mellici call my name from her office, so I headed on in. As I sat down, though I might be imagining it, she looked more relaxed – maybe even nicer. It made me wonder if a lot of her attitude had been based around worrying about her mom and money.

"Alexzandra," she said, flipping through my file. "It looks like you got accepted at a few of the state schools, and at that college in Hawaii," she continued. I nodded.

"Which did you accept?"

I wiggled a little in my chair. This wasn't going to be easy. After a lot of thought, I'd told Mom I thought I should start with community college. Now to tell Mrs. Mellici. I took a deep breath.

"Well," I started, looking down at my hands. "I think that I'm going to go to community college for a year or so—you know, get my generals out of the way, then transfer out to one of these schools."

Then I just waited to see if old sarcastic Mrs. Mellici would come out, tell me how foolish I was. She was silent. I peeked up to see if she'd fainted in shock or something.

She was nodding. "That's not a bad idea, Alexzandra," she said. Now whose turn was it to faint in shock? "Have you considered how to make that work for you?"

I'd called the University of Hawaii and gotten a list of what they would accept, if I did community college for a couple years then transferred. That's the school I wanted to attend; I'd do this so that in the end, I got to go where I wanted to.

"I have," I said, and my voice squeaked. I cleared my throat. "I went over the classes at our community college with Mom, and then actually faxed the list to the administrator at UH. I wanted to be crystal clear what was going to transfer and what was not—and to have it in writing, which they did." Yes, I am my mother's daughter.

Mrs. Mellici nodded and flipped through the pages of my file, making some notes. She took the copies of the in-state applications out of the bracket, and handed them to me. I folded them quickly and dropped them into the wastebasket.

"OK, so this is it," she said. "Sounds like you're on your way, a little different than I would have expected, but you and your parents have obviously thought this through." The way she would have said it before, the 'expected' would have sounded more like she was very disappointed in me. But her voice was all level—more like curious, but OK with the decision. She shut the file and stood up behind her desk, so I stood up, too. Then she put her hand out. I just stared at it for a second, not sure exactly what to do. Then I reached mine out and she took it in hers, even putting her other hand around it. She looked me in the eyes.

"I do know who the Dream Choosers are, you know," she said. I would have stepped back in surprise, but she had my hand in between her two pudgy ones. I'm sure I looked shocked. "Stan Sherman told me. He also said that you're personally responsible for getting this going. I think that's pretty brave. I don't know if you know this, but I'm part of your downline, too." I tried to look surprised—of course, I knew that.

"Last time I saw you, I called your parents to tell them what a mistake they were making; basically what idiots they were," she continued, and I had to suppress a snort. Yeah, Mom v. Mrs. Mellici—I'm seein' it. "I even told some of the other counselors how stupid it was." This soured me up—she did what? Mrs. Mellici let go of my hand when she saw my expression.

"I know, I know, look, I'm telling you this because *I* was the idiot," she said. "Once I realized how something like this could help my husband and me with a problem we were having, I realized I'd burned those bridges, just to have something to be catty about. Once I realized that it really was a professional choice, I felt like I couldn't even talk about it here, because of my own fear of hearing 'I told you so'." She sat back down, looking to the side and shuffling her papers. I just wanted to get out of there, but she obviously wasn't through. This sounded like she was trying to make amends.

"But after a while I had to eat crow, because I had to share that it really is getting us out of a predicament," she continued. I thought for a second, but I couldn't remember if any of the other names on her downline were plaques on the other doors outside her office—except for Principal Melton. "So what I'm saying is, I'm sorry for how I was," she finished—I knew that was my cue to jet.

"Yeah, OK," I nodded, backing out the door and closing it after myself. That had gone different. I mean, not bad, just different. Wait until I texted Stephanie.

Dad's company moved slower than they thought they would, just as Mom had predicted. It was a big undertaking to close his whole division and move it all to Tennessee. Dad finally told them that he wouldn't be moving, but that he'd oversee all the wrapping-up. The week he made that decision was not pleasant around our house; I pretty much stayed in my room. It was like he was watching his life—as he knew it—end. He was freaked about having made a huge mistake. Mom helped him—she was making more at the law firm, plus our checks from the business were growing. Given the various setbacks at Dad's company, it would be located here for a while at least. Until he had to "lock the door and turn over the key," as Mom put it. Then, our MLM business would be his job.

He had good days and bad days about the whole thing, especially as folks that were his peers started to climb the ranks. I think it hurt his pride, seeing people that weren't that good move up just because they agreed to move to Tennessee. I would hear him and Mom talking about it sometimes—and it made me even more determined to avoid that world. Kiyosaki called it the rat race—

people being promoted just because they ran the right pattern in the "maze."

The Friday before finals week, Charlie and I were talking about it in the cafeteria after school before I caught the bus home. He tugged unconsciously at the collar of his new letterman's jacket; it looked like the wool itched. "I still don't get why your dad is doing this," he said, taking a last swig from his bottle of water. "Well," I said, suppressing the urge to scratch his neck for him, "Otherwise, he'd have to go to Tennessee, and Mom and him figure that by the time they shut down all the operations here, plus him doing our business, he won't have to. Which leaves him here, with a lot more free time, too, and no commute. That doesn't sound so bad, does it?"

Charlie leaned in, putting his forearm on the table, spinning the now-empty bottle back and forth with his other hand. "This has me pretty confused," he finally said. "I think Dad is going to talk to your father about this, too." The astonishment was hard to keep out of his voice, and I could see it in his face, too. "*My* dad. Taking career advice from…" then he paused, looked up. "Oh man, I don't mean it like that," he said. "This is not like a diss on your dad, it's just…"

I nodded. We'd been friends—brother and sister practically—for our whole lives, so I got it. The doctor, taking career advice from the middle manager sales guy?

"He just sees where your dad is probably going to be at, compared to him," Charlie continued. "Dad has the clinic, his private practice, board meetings. He's tired a lot. He wants to spend more time with Mom." Charlie kept spinning the water bottle around and around with his long fingers.

"I'm still going to get my math degree and MBA," he said after some silence, almost defiantly. "I still don't get what you're all doing. I get that medicine has changed—the way things are now aren't how they were when Dad got out of med school. And I get that your dad's job moved, so he had to do something different. But I want to be a CEO some day, like Stephanie's dad. I know, sure, he inherited it, but getting an MBA is the path there for someone like me. You can start in the six figures if you go to a good school for your MBA and stay at the top of your class. That's what I'm going for."

I tried to explain that we already owned our own company, so I guess you could say I was already a CEO…but I had a feeling that's not what he meant. I mentioned that people who did this business consistently for a few years got those 'six figures' monthly, not annually, as cash flow income rather not labor and stress income. And they weren't facing a mountain of student loan debt, either. Though it wasn't up to me to change his view, he seemed a little stubborn, especially given his dad's interest now, too. And it's not like I wasn't going to college—I was going with a plan.

It was odd thinking about it all, though. I checked on what Charlie was saying, where people go from high school to college, study business for four years, then get a Master's degree in business in another couple years—then go and get hired at big companies for big bucks without really having "experience." Well, "big bucks" minus the thousands of dollars of debt paying for their education.

Sure, we were learning as we went. We didn't know all the statistics and advanced knowledge that you'd get with an MBA, but we were running our own business already.

Of course, I didn't voice that opinion—I loved Charlie, but I could see our paths were starting to diverge. Not quite as dramatically as with Josh, but it still made me sad.

"That's great for you," I finally said, "but you know, with my hodge-podge of dreams, I don't have a direct path like that." I looked up from watching Charlie mindlessly twirl the water bottle on the table. Stephanie was running up behind him. No time to warn him. She gave Charlie a huge over-the-chair hug, which I could see startled the heck out of him, then came around and rubbed the letter on his jacket. I let out a little snort but kept my mouth closed, so that a big 'ole bray of laughter wouldn't escape at Charlie's expense. You should have seen his face.

"Oooooh, big Letterman," she cooed, sitting down with us in her new tailored Stanford shirt. Yes, she's off to Stanford, just like her dad. Not sure how this exactly works—maybe they'd soon be breaking ground for a Thompson Building on campus, since Steffie's not 4.0 material. "Want a ride?" she asked, making a hitchhiking gesture toward the back parking lot.

"I gotta go to the mailbox," I said, and she shrugged, so I picked up my stuff, nodding to Charlie. He still looked a little shell shocked from the 'Steffie assault.'

"Are we cramming for the chemistry final at your house Saturday?" I asked before I left, and he nodded. "OK I'll be up there around ten," I said, and followed Steffie out the side door toward the lot. School is so odd—you cram to pass a test and get a good grade, but never use or remember any of it. How good of training is this for the Real World? It seems that all school teaches us is to fight against each other instead of working together. Through our business I was learning a whole new reality—I hadn't even realized how programmed I'd been from years of school.

It was getting more and more fun to go to the mailbox. Actually, I didn't go as often, what with studying, finals, graduation prep—OK, parties—and all. Maybe that's why it was fun, because when I did go, there were usually a couple checks. The best were the ones where we didn't know where they came from. I'm not going to say it didn't still seem slow going, but as I heard my mom say once to a friend on the phone, "What if you could retire in four years? Would you put some time and effort into something in that case? And where are you going to be in four years, the way you're going now? The four years are going to pass—whatever you do." That is what we had to keep thinking about—our long-term goals. If you think about it, four years isn't very long at all. Most of my friends would just be starting their first "real" jobs by then. Or maybe moving back in with their folks, if their folks still had a place for them to move back into, that is.

Stephanie came into the mailbox store with me, waiting while I pulled out my key.

"Hello, Miss Stephanie," Juana said, and I turned to look at her incredulously.

"Aloha, Chica!" Stephanie said, doing her little wiggly happy dance, then pointing at box number 30.

"That's Mom's," she said, smiling. I had no idea. "Your Dad explained to my Mom when she started into the business that she should get an address somewhere else. And Juana here," she said, gesturing to the smiling woman who had just grabbed a big handful of mail to stuff into the boxes, "is the best value in town for a private mailbox. I check it for Mom sometimes if she's busy."

Did I mention I had no idea?

Juana headed through the door at the side of the mailboxes as I opened up our box. Nothing, but I thought I should wait around to see if Juana had anything for us in the new mail she was sorting. Stephanie's eyes glittered as she took in all the new merchandise Juana had added since her last visit.

"Why you'd not told me about the business, Miss Alex?" I heard Juana ask from the back of the mailboxes as she sorted the new mail into the appropriate slots. "I wondered about it until Miss Thompson at Box 30 told me." Juana must mean 'Miss Thompson' Stephanie's Mom, not 'Miss Thompson' Stephanie.

"Whoa, my bad, I never thought about it," I said, closing my eyes and shaking my head. What a missed opportunity!

"Miss Thompson told me, then went back to my computer and showed me. Then she told me a lady to talk to—Mrs. Olivia."

OK, that was just funny. That was obviously my mom. Since the mail here all said Dream Choosers, I'm sure Juana never made the connection.

"Mrs. Olivia told me about Eduardo y Maria-Elena Gonzales, that they have a meeting so I went. Miss Thompson came with me too, to be sure I'm OK."

There's no way Mrs. Thompson speaks Spanish, so she obviously wanted to be sure that she was getting the best information to Juana —her prospect. And, as Juana told it, she even went to the meeting to make Juana comfortable.

"So now I know about the business, too. I am doing it, too. Funny not to tell me, you know I'm the best businesswoman, sí?"

That's a fact. With Juana on our team, considering all the mailboxes that she presided over here, we might ultimately have the entire wall in our genealogy. I wasn't sure why I hadn't mentioned it before, but I was sure glad Mrs. Thompson had.

This thing was almost taking on a life of its own. Maybe my text angel was helping.

Chapter Twenty-One

Suddenly—it was graduation. We were seated alphabetically, so I was in the middle back near Stephanie. I watched as my classmates went up to get their diplomas, shake Principal Melton's hand, and do a dance, fist pump, whatever.

I wondered where everyone was going to be in a few years, as I watched Lenardo walk up to get his diploma—a first for his family. I caught their smiling faces, sitting there with their youngest son, right next to my parents, Mrs. Thompson, and Charlie's mom. His dad had been called to the hospital on an emergency. I looked down and gave my head a small shake, smiling at the "Team." A microcosm of Society—the cream, the middle, the base—all shaken up, all together. The way it should be.

Lenardo walked back toward his seat, caught my eye, and winked at me. I thought about all the changes that had gone on for him, especially, that year. His older brother was in jail now—drug possession, big surprise—which had put a little fear into his younger one. I wasn't sure if he'd quit tagging and running with the gang, but he was up there with Lenardo's folks, and in regular clothes, not baggy-saggies and a hoodie, so…maybe.

As Lenardo winked at me, I knew I was looking at someone with the entrepreneurial fire well lit. He was actually going to take some community college classes with me. He didn't have to go to work right away, because his folks were making enough through the MLM that they didn't need him to bring in an income straight after graduation. We'd already kidded that we were going to draw a red line down the middle of the community college campus, and each take a side to introduce people to the opportunity. The thing was—either way, Dream Choosers benefitted. That's the best part. It was win/win for us all. It was so unlike what I kept hearing from my dad, some of the stuff going on at his work…people backstabbing and trying to get ahead on the backs of someone else. In a way, that's what I realized we'd also learned in school—you were getting great grades, you were fine. You weren't getting great grades, you sucked. People worked to memorize and spew out then forget everything they learned to scramble to be at the top; to be 'over' the ones who didn't quite make it. We were definitely not shown how to help someone take a step up—how to make mistakes work for you—how to feel OK about asking questions. That asking questions didn't make you 'stupid,' it helped you learn, and not make them again.

    I stood up—it was time for my row to head down towards Mr. Melton. We inched forward, adjusting our headboards and tassels.

    I was learning a lot by talking about the business, especially about mistakes and questions. Folks like Mr. Sherman had started with a lot of questions. They wanted to understand how it worked. Then there were folks who didn't want to ask questions because they didn't want to look 'stupid.' They'd either sign up and do nothing, or wouldn't sign up, because 'it just wasn't for them'—without even really checking it out. Like my bus driver Doug. Or Josh. Or Charlie.

    I smiled at Mom and Dad in the crowd as I got closer to the podium where Mr. Melton would shake our hands, hand the diploma over, then turn the tassel from right to left for each student to signify going from candidate to graduate. Dad shot me a thumbs up. They were beaming, as were Charlie's mom, Mr. and Mrs. Gonzales, and Mrs. Thompson, who actually looked a lot better than she ever had, and not just because her hair was a healthy, shiny chestnut brown now. Why had she done that whole blonde thing to herself? What a mistake—but maybe that's what she'd thought she needed to do. Not anymore.

I inched forward—just a few more steps before I got to the podium. I thought some more about questions. Mom and Dad actually had started having team calls, just like Jordan Adler and Sophie. The main thing was to answer questions. I'd mentioned to Mom that I was finding some people didn't want to ask questions, and then would just avoid me. So we gathered up the questions that most people asked, and Mom and Dad answered them at the beginning of each of their calls. We tried to make it safe and easy to get people to ask stuff—if they don't ask, you can't know how to help them.

I wish I'd understood this sooner in my life. I would have sat in the front more in class—like Lenardo—and asked questions when I didn't get something. I would have cared a lot less about what people thought, and gained a better understanding of what I didn't 'get.' We never really had to understand what we'd gotten wrong—we just got it wrong, that's bad, move on, memorize more, don't look stupid or slow. I wasn't quite sure how this was supposed to help us with our futures, but all the kids that now sort of looked down their noses at me when I said I was going to community college obviously felt that another four, six, eight, whatever years of the same, was going to get them the good life. Hmm.

Dad totally embarrassed me with one of his two-handed whistles when I hit the podium. OK, *seriously*? But then I thought about Josh. When he'd crossed the stage, he'd hammed it up with Mr. Melton and folks laughed, but no one was out in the audience for him.

After graduation, Mom and Dad gave me the OK to stay out and party, even giving me the keys to the car. I had to call if I drank though, so that one of them could come get me. We had a blast—Stephanie had convinced her dad to spring for a seriously rockin' party at their house. Everyone was there—even Charlie. Stef was in her element as hostess, though she tried to get me to play Keymeister to be sure no one left in bad shape. I declined, and stuck to the virgin daiquiris the bartender whipped up, myself.

Mrs. Thompson even let Mr. Thompson come, and you could see he was trying to figure her out. With her new relaxed demeanor and shaking her thick mane of luxurious chestnut brown hair as she laughed and joked, it was obvious she wasn't particularly concerned about what he thought. He even kind of flirted with her, and she was smilingly sassy back. I guess *that's* where Steffie got it from. It was like, as soon as she started to have fun and be independent, he was sniffing back around to see what he might have missed.

When the party started to turn a little rowdy, I figured I'd better split before people started getting thrown in the pool. I sought out Steffie to say good-bye and collect my keys.

On the way out, I looked up from the Thompson's wrap-around front porch. The stars were just coming out, and I thought forward, doing a little happy dance like Steffie's silly one, then looked back over my shoulder, a little embarrassed, to be sure no one had caught me. We had met our goal with time to spare. In a couple months I'd be seeing those same stars—over Hawaii!

Chapter Twenty-Two

"Isn't this fantastic?" Sophie said, lying next to me on a chaise on the beach. I still couldn't believe I was here.

"The best," I murmured from under my big floppy hat. I took a sip from the tropical drink one of the cabana boys had brought me.

Mom, Dad and I had arrived the day before. Sophie and I were sharing a room; that way Mom and Dad had a little time to themselves.

I'd turned 18 just before we made the trip, and Mom and Dad had officially, legally added me to the Dream Choosers entity. It didn't mean that much to me; it wasn't like they were going to fleece me out of anything, but it made me feel totally amazing.

During the time between graduation and our trip, I'd started making some calls to our downline when Mom and Dad were at work. I wanted to be sure everyone was doing OK, seeing if they had any questions or if they needed me to help with three-way calls or anything. I wanted everyone to know they were supported, just like Sophie had done for us. She was just as available as always when we ran up against something that we didn't understand. Also, after talking it over with her and my folks, I started holding some Lunch and Learn meetings about the business. This way our team could bring guests, and I could answer any questions. I hung out at Starbucks or the local sandwich shop, and called it "work." I felt like a total executive, especially considering I was always surrounded by self-employed adults busily working away. By their age, I planned to be working a lot less than they obviously were!

"What are Charlie and Stephanie doing before college?" Sophie asked, adjusting her chaise so that she could look out at the ocean.

"Charlie's working for his mom, restocking her store this summer, and Stef's a hostess at their club." I thought about it for a second. Pretty different than me, sitting here on an all-expenses-paid trip to Hawaii that our "job" had sent us to.

"Doesn't sound like much fun," she said, and I knew she was thinking what I was thinking. Yeah, I know, we shouldn't gloat. Just a bit though, OK?

"What'd you guys do before I got here?" she asked. She'd just arrived that morning.

"Mom, Dad and I headed out to UH after unpacking yesterday to check it out in person," I said. Dad had this file on Hawaii from his ferry-riding days, just as I'd imagined he would. We'd also gotten some sightseeing done before visiting the campus. "And Dad was really proud to be able to show us some 'hidden treasures' he'd collected info on during his commutes." I remembered how his eyes got all shiny to be able to put his file to use.

"Oh, so you hit the campus?" Sophie asked. "How'd it look?"

"The admissions director showed us around personally—I'd spent so much time with her on the phone making sure about what would transfer from the community college, it was almost like she was an old friend," I said, smiling. "She looked just like I thought she would. Oh—and she's part of our team, too." Sophie raised an eyebrow, so I continued. "Yeah, a few months ago, when she asked why I was so concerned about the transfer credits since I'd gotten accepted already, I had to explain what I was up to and why I was deferring enrollment. And she was interested. And she checked it out. And she joined."

"Starting the team before you actually get here," Sophie said. "Smart." I laughed.

Sophie pulled out her magazine and flicked through it; I picked up my phone from the table that sat between us, and swiped it open to text Stephanie as I'd promised her I'd do. I was pretty sure she'd be happy for me, but I thought about her in that stuffy Club, and closed the screen without typing, putting it under my book so it wouldn't cook in the sun.

I also thought about my text angel. I checked in sometimes—just to be sure she was still there—but the texts were mainly "Howz by u?" "LML how u?" "LML2!" It was almost like my relationship with Sophie—a friend who was there to help, but who I didn't really need to ask anymore. I thought about texting, just to say thanks basically for getting me to Hawaii, but it still felt weird so I left it alone.

Mom and Dad had gone off, leaving me in Sophie's capable hands, as Mom had said. I mean, I was 18. Hello. I have my own capable hands. But whatever, and it was actually really fun to be with Sophie.

"Do you want to go in for a dip?" I asked her. If we wanted to swim, now was the time to do it; she was having a get-together up at the pool area with all her team members that had won the trip, and we'd want to shower and change beforehand. In fact, since people from our Dream Choosers Team under her, like the Gonzaleses and Mr. Sherman (yes, really!) had won the trip also, Mom and Dad had some special stuff to present to them beforehand and had asked them to show up 20 minutes early.

Instead of answering my question, Sophie rolled out of her reclining chair toward me, just as I swung out of mine toward her. I knocked the table over in the sand getting my balance; she fell straight back in her chaise with a thump. We both burst out laughing. One of the cabana boys came flying.

We couldn't stop giggling. "I'm not so sure it's safe when we're in the same place, Alex."

I righted the table, as the attendant arrived. "Don't worry about that, Miss," he said, picking up the now-empty glass with its crushed umbrella. "I'll bring you another one. If you ladies are going for a swim, it'll all be set when you get back."

We were still giggling, but Sophie grabbed my hand and we ran toward the waves as the attendant kicked some sand over the spot where the drink had spilled, and straightened our towels. "Race ya!" she said and the sand flew out from under our feet as we sped toward the sparkling water.

I showered, then changed for the pre-meeting with our team. Sophie let me go first, and was just heading in herself as I fastened my earrings. "So, who's going to bring in the first team made up totally of cabana boys?" she said, laughing. Actually, I had been thinking about that—I was going to mention it to Lenardo when I went down to our team get-together. They seemed to be in the same sort of situation the Gonzaleses had been in—working a lot for not much—and I bet hearing the Gonzales' story would get them thinking.

"I wonder if they can envision lying and drinking a mai tai, instead of trying to clean up when Idiot Girl knocks her drink off the table," I laughed, then froze. The table. "Oh my gosh!" I said, loud enough for Sophie, with a towel wrapped around her head and another around her body, to poke her head around the corner of the bathroom.

"What?" she said. I was furiously pawing through my beach bag. Book....towel...sunglasses...

"Oh man—my phone!"

She looked puzzled.

"Remember, everything flew off the table. My phone was under my book."

"I'm sure it's down there," she said. "Look, just go to the beach station where the guys go to bring up the drink orders and stuff. I'm sure they have a lost and found."

I nodded, grabbed my room key, slipped on my sandals, and sped out the door.

"What should I tell my folks?" I whined to Lenardo as we lay poolside after Sophie's shindig. A balmy breeze ruffled the palm fronds above our heads. Lenardo lazily fingered the necklace with the Numero Uno charm that Mom and Dad had presented to him at our Dream Choosers Team meeting. It was actually kind of cheesy, even though it was gold, but he'd immediately put it on and told them he would wear it proudly.

"Well, you ask me, that phone was getting old anyways," he said, staring up at the darkening sky. I think that he was still a little shocked by all the attention. My folks had made a big fuss over him and his parents, too, during their presentation. And then at Sophie's party, he'd drawn the attention from some of the women on Sophie's team! That's why we were lying under the trees at the back of the huge pool and ponds area—he wasn't exactly hiding… well, not *exactly*. "You should just get a new one. Does your phone have a security code?" I nodded. "Then I wouldn't worry. And besides—a new phone is a business deduction." He smiled over at me as I rolled my eyes.

I'd gone down to the beach as Sophie had suggested, but no one had the phone. Well, at least now I could explain why I hadn't texted friends back home, especially Stephanie. I'd felt bad about the idea of basically saying that I was having the time of my life—being treated like an adult, and not even just an adult, but as a real *businessperson*—while they were working their summers away. Now I had an excuse for the silence. Lenardo and I had talked about it, and both of us marveled that, in network marketing, age didn't really count as much as results. It was cool. He had changed; he now gave off this totally radiant energy. The Lenardo I knew from school – good looking, but a bit shy and bookish – had transformed.

"Yeah, guess you're right," I said to Lenardo about my phone. We lay there silently, the breeze ruffling his hair and the edge of my bright white beach towel.

Jordan Adler, who of course had also won the trip, actually had stopped by Sophie's get-together; in fact, when Sophie had reminded Mr. Adler that he'd met us, back when we'd first gone to check out the company he smiled at me, then nodded over to where my mom and dad were talking with Mr. Sherman and said, "How are your folks doing?" I realized that not only did he remember me from that very short meeting in front of the stage ages ago, he even remembered who my folks were. No wonder he was so good at what he did.

I lazily looked out past our feet, then squinted. In the distance next to one of the beachside fire pits, I saw a group; it was Lenardo's folks, with—yes—a bunch of the cabana boys listening intently. I had to smile.

"I still can't believe this," Lenardo said. I totally knew what he meant. He was quiet for a minute, then said, "I really need to say thank you. If you hadn't asked for my opinion all those months ago, I…my family wouldn't be here."

"It's no big deal," I started to say.

"It is to us," he interrupted. "Seriously, Alex, you've changed our lives. Thank you."

Epilogue

"OK, you guys are embarrassing me," I shouted, turning on my heel in the wet sand. Then I just had to peek back over my shoulder and laughed, shaking my head. Mom popped up in the waist-deep water, her hair over her face, spitting and laughing. Dad and Sam were still holding the surfboard they'd been trying to get her to balance on, with that surprised "O!" look on their faces. She'd knelt up triumphantly, given a fist-pump, and tumbled off the back. Hilarious.

Sam smiled at me and winked, his dark brown eyes twinkling. Then he turned back to Mom. "We'll get you up there, Olivia. No worries," he said. I'd met him on my first day at the University of Hawaii, almost like how I met Sophie—we'd slammed into each other standing up from our chairs at the UH student orientation meeting. Grace. My middle name.

"My hands are prunes, I'm going to sit this one out," I said as I headed back up the beach toward the chaises. Dad and Sam waved, then turned their attention back to Mom. She was totally determined to do this.

I thought back to that day a few years ago, when we were lying on the living room sofas, dreaming about what we might be able to do if we got a "B-Business" to fly. Shockingly, Mom had wanted to learn to surf. She'd actually tried it when we won the expenses-paid trip to Hawaii when we first were starting out—they were even staying here at that same hotel. But she'd sucked; she was too worried about how she looked to the others in the class. Now, with Dad and Sam helping her, I was sure she'd be relaxed enough to live out her dream.

Just like me, I realized. I reached our chairs and sipped on my drink. I was totally living my dream! Brilliant, fun Hawaiian boyfriend, happy healthy parents, cash flow, a business I loved introducing people to, and now I'm at my first choice college. Our business wasn't likely to "save the world"—but, once I finished my research and studies at UH, I just might.

Mom's screams of laughter drifted toward me as I saw her kneel up for a second on the surfboard before face-planting into the water. Sam and Dad burst out laughing, but of course cut it short as soon as she surfaced. They could only hold it for a couple seconds before they both blew up with their held-in laughter. Mom, looking a tiny bit like a drowned cat, scowled first, but their infectious laughter hit her, too.

What a great life.

I took another long pull from the cool, fruity drink. Then I reached for the sunscreen from the table, and put a bit more on my arms, legs and feet. I'd wait for Sam to massage it into my back and shoulders I thought, smiling.

I moved my shoulders back and forth on the rolled-up beach towel an attendant had brought over. Then I picked up my sunhat from the table, removing the gorgeous Marta Howell blister pearl pendant Mom and Dad had given me for my 21st birthday yesterday, so it wouldn't leave a white mark in my tan. Content, I leaned back to doze in the beautiful tropical sun.

The late-afternoon breezes gusted unexpectedly over the sand. It bent my sunhat slightly sideways, and caught in the pages of the magazine at my feet. I opened my eyes to see the breeze speeding through the pages, and I reached to catch the magazine before it blew off the chaise. I missed grabbing the magazine, but in the lunge, I managed to knock the table over. I sat up as the attendant came running. Slick. How clumsy can one girl be?

Luckily, my folks and Sam hadn't caught my graceful performance. I stood up, wiping sand off the magazine. The attendant righted the table and knelt down to pick up the ice and put it back in the glass with the smashed little umbrella straw to take it away.

"This yours?" he said. I looked over. Then I took off my sunglasses and really *looked*. He was holding a cell phone. There was a line of black stones with one rhinestone on the top. My stomach did a flip. "Something wrong?" the attendant asked, concerned.

"No, no nothing," I said, and picked it up. I looked blankly at it. *No, it couldn't be.* But what if it was? No way would it have power after three years. I pushed the button.

It turned right on. Full battery. I felt a chill run down my back, even though it was a warm tropical day. I stared at the phone, slowly typing in my old security code. Yep.

I just stood there for what seemed like a very, very long time. I could hear Mom's screaming laughter, but it sounded far away. I stared down the beach, calculating…figuring out what day it was… and what time back home. Day after my birthday. About 2:00 in the afternoon—right before I used to have English, Senior Year in high school. Yep. I could almost hear the locker doors banging. I nodded. Punched in the numbers. Punched in the message:

YDKM but WDR
U can hv ur drms n $$ n safety
Uni z NTOW

Staring at my boyfriend and my folks, rough housing it up in the water, I felt very still, very silent. I held the phone. The heat from it being buried in the sand warmed my palm. The attendant said something else to me, but I just nodded and he went away to get me another glass. I could hear blood whooshing in my ears. No way.

The phone pinged. I didn't even have to look. But I did.

WDYM

List of Resources

If you are interested in any of the authors mentioned in this book or about network marketing in general, here are some great resources for further information:

- Robert Kiyosaki: RichDad.com
- Zig Ziglar: Ziglar.com
- Jordan Adler: BeachMoney.com
- Networking Times: NetworkingTimes.com
- SUCCESS Magazine: Success.com
- Tommy Wyatt and Curtis Lewsey: AppreciationMarketing.com
- Curtis Lewsey: DormRoomWealth.com
- Jim Rohn: JimRohn.com
- Tom "Big Al" Schreiter: FortuneNow.com
- Eric Worre: NetworkMarketingPro.com
- Adam Packard: AdamPackard.com
- additional resources can be found at DreamChoosers.com/Resources

In the spirit of giving back, I am delighted to donate a portion of the author proceeds to worthy charitable organizations benefiting teen entrepreneurs. Any information on such organizations is always welcome.

> "We make a living by what we get, but we make a life by what we give." – Winston Churchill

About The Author

Sandy Shepard has more degrees than any sane person should. She has an Associates, a Bachelors, a quad-major Masters, and a Doctor of Laws degree. She is also a Certified Business Success Coach, and holds certificates in such diverse areas as authentic movement study and practice, therapeutic bodywork, and advanced bartending.

She worked in the Business Affairs/Legal department at LucasArts, as well as software companies such as Mindscape, Broderbund, Mattel, and Scene7, winding up as general counsel. But everything changed when she found the right network marketing company.

Information about her two other books can be found at *BeABondGirl.com*. General MLM information can be found at *DreamChoosers.com;* information on her chosen MLM can be found at *BestLifestyleToday.com*. She lives in Marin County, California with her husband and enjoys speaking, training and traveling internationally.

www.ingramcontent.com/pod-product-compliance
Lightning Source LLC
Chambersburg PA
CBHW061509180526
45171CB00001B/107